STRANGE STUDIES FROM LIFE

STRANGE STUDIES FROM LIFE

"*His mother appeared in the witness-box.*" Illustration by Sidney Paget for "*The Love Affair of George Vincent Parker*" as it appeared in the STRAND magazine for April 1901.

Strange Studies from Life

AND OTHER NARRATIVES

The Complete True Crime Writings
of
SIR ARTHUR CONAN DOYLE

Selected and Edited by Jack Tracy
Introduction by Peter Ruber
Illustrated by Sidney Paget

GASLIGHT PUBLICATIONS
BLOOMINGTON, INDIANA • 1988

ISBN: 0-934468-49-4

Library of Congress
Catalogue Card No. 82-83684

Printed in the United States of America

First printing: April 1988
Second printing: June 1992

GASLIGHT PUBLICATIONS
112 East Second
Bloomington, Indiana 47401

The cases dealt with in this series of studies of criminal psychology are taken from the actual history of crime, though occasionally names have been changed where their retention might cause pain to surviving relatives.

Contents

"It was the footprint of a man, dimly outlined in blood upon the wooden floor." Illustration by Sidney Paget for "The Debatable Case of Mrs. Emsley" as it appeared in the STRAND *magazine for May 1901.*

Introduction

ANY YEARS AGO, I had a dream, one of those typical childhood dreams that are filled with wonderful notions at the point of occurrence. When I awoke, the dream had vanished, like one of the silvery-winged faeries one envisions beside a babbling mountain brook. For hours afterward, the last fragment danced wildly in my head, and I sought vainly to piece my dream together so I could relive that one moment of youthful ecstacy.

Much time, it is said, is wasted dreaming, but who among us is without the power to dream? I doubt if anyone is so unromantic that he cannot spend at least a few conscious moments daily in a dreamlike trance, removed from the world around him. Dreams have an uncanny way of invading our lives when we least expect it. They lead us to the very threshold of lands both near and far. We travel vast distances of time and space in a fleeting second, and return at will if we are not pleased with what we dream. In dreams we can, with the same ease, be all the things which in life we could never hope to be, or duplicate the heroics of our storybook giants.

Each person in his own way is like Salathiel, the Wandering Jew, who, as we are told, has lived through all the ages and will continue to live throughout all the years to come, watching the centuries unfold. How we would wish we could trade places with him!

Writers are the greatest dreamers of all: their dreams remain the symbols of their unguarded moments when, filled with inspiration, they composed with pen and ink the words so well loved by succeeding generations. But we love only those books in which the characters and events could be in direct association to our own dreams. The vicarious experience is not to be matched by coins of the realm.

Writers are the only dreamers who share their dreams with others. One of the great dreammakers was Sir Arthur Conan Doyle, the master Victorian story-teller. When we read his books, the narration comes alive, and suddenly we behold his image before us. It is as if he were telling the stories from his own lips, and we not merely reading the words from the printed page. His tales of knighthood in flower, of swash-buckling men and women more beautiful than artists could re-create, are found in the historical volumes of *Sir Nigel, The White Company, Uncle Bernac,* the *Adventures* and *Exploits of Brigadier Gerard.* And the fantasy novels: *The Land of Mist, The Lost World, The Poison Belt,* and the many volumes of short stories. There were also his tales of sinister nights in London town. Do you recall how often we followed the shadow of the man with the Inverness cape and deerstalker, either on a merry chase down the River Thames or in a racing hansom cab? Yes, I speak of Mr. Sherlock Holmes, perhaps Conan Doyle's greatest dream; the societies that honour this fictional sleuth today attest the living tribute of this dream.

Mr. Holmes never wore a deerstalker — we have Sir

Arthur's word for that — nor smoked that pipe we see in
movies and latter-day illustrations, that curious curved
affair which we have come to associate with him. These
two items were adapted by William Gillette in his
dramatic portrayal of this Victorian personage. When
Gillette was asked why he smoked the curved pipe on
stage, he replied that it rested more firmly in his mouth
and enabled him to deliver his lines with greater ease.
Perhaps these were the touches Holmes needed to give
him "life" — or don't you agree? Holmes is the symbol
of Conan Doyle's belief in justice, and we never
remember one and forget the other.

What causes us to emerge from our dreams?
According to the eminent scholar Vincent Starrett, the
cause is the "Persons from Porlock." Mr. Starrett
writes:

They are so amiable, most of them. They mean so well. It is
perhaps the worst feature of the entire conspiracy that they
are so innocent of malice. If their intentions were malicious,
an end to their activities might be accomplished with the
object nearest at hand — a walking stick, or a flower pot, or
even a handy chair. Too often, however, the interrupter is
somebody who really should know better — somebody who
would be himself the first to shudder at a knock of interruptions on his door. . . . Where is this Porlock that seems to
have so many inhabitants? The place has no frontiers. Its
history is the stupendous history of Time. . . . In kindness
perhaps he comes, the last and most formidable of his
caravan. His business brooks no delay. By him indeed are
we detained above an hour.

The history of Time tells us he invades the privacy of
writers more significantly, perhaps, than we acknowl-

edge his invasion into ours. The history of Time is also the written record of his interruptions. . .

One came to Samuel Taylor Coleridge as he was writing the 54th line of *Kubla Khan,* a narrative poem he had conceived in its entirety in a dream. He awoke from his opium sleep and began to record this vision, similar to the dreamlike inspirations experienced by Edgar Allan Poe. Then the fateful knock on the front door. When he returned, his dream had vanished. The fragment that remains is but one of many that plagued Coleridge in his debt-ridden life.

And then there was Charles Dickens. He met his Person from Porlock as he was balancing the ink-stained slab of oak that served as his writing table. He died, never completing *The Mystery of Edwin Drood.* The Drood story is still very profound to the thinning ranks of literary scholars who for the last century and more have written penetrating studies on how the mystery might have been unravelled had Dickens lived to complete it. The public is grateful, however, to Wilkie Collins, friend and collaborator of the deceased, for writing the conclusion for publication.

And then F. Arbuthnot Wilson. Perhaps you know him better as Grant Allen, popular novelist of the Victorian era, and creator of Colonel Clay, first of the fictional criminals. The Person from Porlock visited his deathbed in 1899, and his novel *Hilda Wade* was left unfinished. Conan Doyle lived nearby and, in an unusual act of literary friendship, completed the book and saw its posthumous publication in 1900.

Conan Doyle himself was soon to be paid a visit from this Person from Porlock. It was in the early days of 1901. He had just returned from South Africa. For months to come, he was to be plagued by illness. He began to write a monthly feature for the *Strand* magazine, concerning true-life crime, called "Strange Studies from Life." A champion of human rights and a staunch defender of justice, Doyle was seriously engaged in not merely reporting the facts about several notable crimes of decades past, but in treating them as a series of studies of criminal psychology of which the moral is more full of warning than that of many Sunday sermons. He planned, according to his contract with Sir George Newnes, publisher of the *Strand,* at least twelve stories. But all that ever appeared were "The Holocaust of Manor Place," "The Love Affair of George Vincent Parker," and "The Debatable Case of Mrs. Emsley," in the March, April, and May 1901 issues.

His visitor from Porlock came at the end of March. His illness was no better, so he left his notes and joined B. Fletcher Robinson, a journalist friend, at a country club near Cromer, by the North Sea. There he rested and played some golf. In the evenings, by the fire of their sitting room, Robinson related the legends of demons that were supposed to lurk among the stone quarries of the Dartmoor district of Devonshire. Doyle's Person from Porlock came in the guise of a spectral hound and the curse of the family Baskerville, and a week later they arrived at Robinson's ancestral estate at Dartmoor. And so Doyle began to write the greatest of Gothic detective novels, *The Hound of the Baskervilles.* He never returned to the "Strange Studies from Life." We cannot hold it against this Person from Porlock, however. He took away with one hand and gave us with the other — perhaps in the irony of fate balancing the eternal proposition of life.

— PETER RUBER

STRANGE STUDIES FROM LIFE

"*Her bundle of love-letters upon her lap.*" *Illustration by Sidney Paget for "The Holocaust of Manor Place" as it appeared in the* STRAND *magazine for March 1901.*

The Holocaust of
Manor Place

IN the study of criminal psychology, one is forced to the conclusion that the most dangerous of all types of mind is that of the inordinately selfish man. He is a man who has lost his sense of proportion. His own will and his own interest have blotted out for him the duty which he owes to the community. Impulsiveness, jealousy, vindictiveness are the fruitful parents of crime, but the insanity of selfishness is the most dangerous and also the most unlovely of them all. Sir Willoughby Patterne, the eternal type of all egoists, may be an amusing and harmless character as long as things go well with him, but let him be thwarted — let the thing which he desires be withheld from him, and the most monstrous results may follow.

Huxley has said that a man in this life is for ever playing a game with an unseen opponent, who only makes his presence felt by exacting a penalty every time one makes a mistake in the game. The player who makes the mistake of selfishness may have a terrible forfeit to pay — but the unaccountable thing in the rules is that some, who are only spectators of his game, may have to help him in the paying. Read the story of William Godfrey Youngman, and see how difficult it is to understand the rules under which these penalties are exacted. Learn also from it that selfishness is no harmless peccadillo, but that it is an evil root from which the most monstrous growths may spring.

About forty miles to the south of London, and close to the rather *passé* watering-place of Tunbridge Wells, there lies the little townlet of Wadhurst. It is situated within the borders of Sussex at a point which is close to the confines of Kent. The country is a rich pastoral one, and the farmers are a flourishing race, for they are near enough to the Metropolis to take advantage of its mighty appetite. Among these farmers there lived, in the year 1860, one Streeter, the master of a small homestead and the father of a fair daughter, Mary Wells Streeter.

Mary was a strong, robust girl, some twenty years of age, skilled in all country work, and with some knowledge also of the town, for she had friends up there, and above all she had one friend, a young man of twenty-five, whom she had met upon one of her occasional visits, and who had admired her so that he had actually come down to Wadhurst after her, and had spent a night under her father's roof. The father had expressed no disapprobation of the suitor, a brisk, masterful young fellow, a little vague in his description of his own occupation and prospects, but an excellent fireside companion. And so it came about that the deep, town-bred William Godfrey Youngman became engaged to the simple, country-bred Mary Wells Streeter, William knowing all about Mary, but Mary very little about William.

July the 29th of that year fell upon a Sunday, and Mary sat in the afternoon in the window of the farmhouse parlour, with her bundle of love-letters upon her lap, reading them again and yet again. Outside was the

little square of green lawn, fringed with the homely
luxuriance of an English country garden, the high
hollyhocks, the huge nodding sunflowers, the bushes of
fuchsia, and the fragrant clumps of sweet William.
Through the open lattice came the faint, delicate scent
of the lilac and the long, low droning of the bees. The
farmer had lain down to the plethoric sleep of the
Sunday afternoon, and Mary had the room to herself.

There were fifteen love-letters in all: some shorter,
some longer, some wholly delightful, some with scattered business allusions, which made her wrinkle her
pretty brows. There was this matter of the insurance,
for example, which had cost her lover so much anxiety
until she had settled it. No doubt he knew more of the
world than she, but still it was strange that she, so
young and so hale, should be asked and again asked to
prepare herself for death. Even in the flush of her love
those scattered words struck a chill to her heart.

"Dearest girl," he had written, "I have filled up the
paper now, and took it to the life insurance office, and
they will write to Mrs. James Bone to-day to get an
answer on Saturday. So you can go to the office with
me before two o'clock on Monday." And then again,
only two days later, he had begun his letter: "You
promised me faithfully over and over again, and I
expect you to keep your promise, that you would be
mine, and that your friends would not know it until we
were married; but now, dearest Mary, if you will only
let Mrs. James Bone write to the insurance office at
once and go with me to have your life insured on
Monday morning next!"

So ran the extracts from the letters, and they per-
plexed Mary as she read them. But it was all over now,
and he should mingle business no longer with his love,

for she had yielded to his whim, and the insurance for £100 had been duly effected. It had cost her a quarterly payment of 10*s*. 4*d.*, but it had seemed to please him, and so she would think of it no more.

There was a click of the garden gate, and, looking up, she saw the porter from the station coming up the path with a note in his hand. Seeing her at the window, he handed it in and departed, slily smiling, a curious messenger of Cupid in his corduroys and clumping boots — a messenger of a grimmer god than Cupid, had he but known it. She had eagerly torn it open, and this was the message that she read: —

16, Manor Place, Newington, S.E.
Saturday night, July 28th.

My beloved Polly, —

I have posted one letter to you this afternoon, but I find that I shall not have to go to Brighton to-morrow as I have had a letter from there with what I wanted inside of it, so, my dear girl, I have quite settled my business now and I am quite ready to see you now, therefore I send this letter to you. I will send this to London Bridge Station to-morrow morning by 6.30 o'clock and get the guard to take it to Wadhurst Station, to give it to the porter there, who will take it to your place. I can only give the guard something, so you can give the man who brings this a small sum. I shall expect to see you, my dear girl, on Monday morning by the first train. I will await your coming at London Bridge Station. I know the time the train arrives — a quarter to ten o'clock. I have promised to go to my uncle's to-morrow, so I cannot come down; but I will go with you home on Monday night or first thing Tuesday morning, and so return here again Tuesday night, to be ready to go anywhere on Wednesday; but you know all that I have told you, and I now expect that you will come up on Monday morning, when I shall be able to manage things as I expect to do. Excuse more now, my dearest Mary. I shall now go to bed to be up early to-morrow to take this letter. Bring or burn all your letters, my dear girl. Do not forget; and with kind love and respects to all I now sum up, awaiting to see you Monday morning a quarter to ten o'clock. — Believe, me, ever your loving, affectionate,

WILLIAM GODFREY YOUNGMAN.

A very pressing invitation, this, to a merry day in town; but there were certainly some curious phrases in it. What did he mean by saying that he would manage things as he expected to do? And why should she burn or bring her love-letters? There, at least, she was determined to disobey this masterful suitor who always "expected" in so authoritative a fashion that she would do this or that. Her letters were much too precious to be disposed of in this off-hand fashion. She packed them back, sixteen of them now, into the little tin box in which she kept her simple treasures, and then ran to meet her father, whose step she heard upon the stairs, to tell him of her invitation and the treat which awaited her to-morrow.

At a quarter to ten next morning, William Godfrey Youngman was waiting upon the platform of London Bridge Station to meet the Wadhurst train, which was bringing his sweetheart up to town. No observer glancing down the straggling line of loiterers would have picked him out as the man whose name and odious fame would, before another day was passed, be household words to all the three million dwellers in London. In person he was of a goodly height and build, but commonplace in his appearance, and with a character which was only saved from insignificance through the colossal selfishness, tainted with insanity, which made him conceive that all things should bend before his needs and will. So distorted was his outlook that it even seemed to him that, if he wished people to be deceived, they must be deceived, and that the weakest device or excuse, if it came from him, would pass unquestioned.

He had been a journeyman tailor, as his father was before him, but, aspiring beyond this, he had sought and obtained a situation as footman to Dr. Duncan, of Covent Garden. Here he had served with credit for some time, but had finally resigned his post and had returned to his father's house, where for some time he had been living upon the hospitality of his hard-worked parents. He had talked vaguely of going into farming, and it was doubtless his short experience of Wadhurst, with its sweet-smelling kine and Sussex breezes, which had put the notion into his Cockney head.

But now the train rolls in, and there at a third-class window is Mary Streeter with her pink country cheeks, the pinker at the sight of her waiting lover. He takes her bag, and they walk down the platform together amongst the crinolined women and baggy-trousered men whose pictures make the London of this date more strange to us than that of last century. He lives at Walworth, in South London, and a straw-strewn omnibus outside the station conveys them almost to the door. It was eleven o'clock when they arrived at Manor Place, where Youngman's family resided.

The household arrangements at Manor Place were peculiar. The architect having not yet evolved the flat in England, the people had attained the same result in another fashion. The tenant of a two-storied house resided upon the ground floor, and then sub-let his first and second floors to other families. Thus, in the present instance, Mr. James Bevan occupied the ground, Mr. and Mrs. Beard the first, and the Youngman family the second, of the various floors of No. 16, Manor Place. The ceilings were thin, and the stairs were in common, so it may be imagined that each family took a lively interest in the doings of its neighbour. Thus Mr. and Mrs. Beard of the first floor were well aware that young Youngman had brought his sweetheart home, and were even able, through half-closed doors, to catch a glimpse of her, and to report that his manner towards her was affectionate.

It was not a very large family to which he introduced her. The father departed to his tailoring at five o'clock every morning and returned at ten at night. There remained only the mother, a kindly, anxious, hard-working woman, and two younger sons aged eleven and seven. At eleven o'clock the boys were at school and the mother alone. She welcomed her country visitor, eyeing her meanwhile and summing up up as a mother would do when first she met the woman whom her son was likely to marry. They dined together, and then the two set forth to see something of the sights of London.

No record has been left of what the amusements were to which this singular couple turned: he with a savage, unrelenting purpose in his heart; she wondering at his abstracted manner, and chattering country gossip with the shadow of death already gathering thickly over her. One little incident has survived. One Edward Spicer, a bluff, outspoken publican who kept the Green Dragon in Bermondsey Street, knew Mary Streeter and her father. The couple called together at the inn, and Mary presented her lover. We have no means of knowing what repellent look mine host may have observed in the young man's face, or what malign trait he may have detected in his character, but he drew the girl aside and whispered that it was better for her to take a rope and hang herself in his skittle-alley than to marry such a man as that—a warning which seems to have met the same fate as most other warnings received by maidens of their lovers.

In the evening, they went to the theatre together to see one of Macready's tragedies. How could she know, as she sat in the crowded pit, with her silent lover at her side, that her own tragedy was far grimmer than any upon the stage? It was eleven o'clock before they were back once more at Manor Place.

The hard-working tailor had now returned, and the household all supped together. Then they had to be divided for the night between the two bedrooms, which were all the family possessed. The mother, Mary, and the boy of seven occupied the front one. The father slept on his own board in the back one, and in a bed beside him lay the young man and the boy of eleven. So they settled down to sleep, as commonplace a family as any in London, with little thought that within a day the attention of all the great city would be centred upon those two dingy rooms and upon the fates of their inmates.

The father woke in the very early hours, and saw in the dim light of the dawn the tall figure of his son standing in white beside his bed. To some sleepy remark that he was stirring early the youth muttered an excuse and lay down once more. At five, the tailor rose to his endless task, and at twenty minutes past he went down the stair and closed the hall door behind him. So passed away the only witness, and all that remains is conjecture and circumstantial evidence. No one will ever know the exact details of what occurred, and for the purpose of the chronicler it is as well, for such details will not bear to be too critically examined. The motives and mind of the murderer are of perennial interest to every student of human nature, but the vile record of his actual brutality may be allowed to pass away when the ends of justice have once been served by their recital.

I have said that on the floor under the Youngmans there lived a couple named Beard. At half-past five, a little after the time when the tailor had closed the hall door behind him, Mrs. Beard was disturbed by a sound which she took to be from children running up and down and playing. There was a light patter of feet on the floor above. But, as she listened, it struck her that there was something unusual in this romping at so early an hour, so she nudged her husband and asked him for his opinion. Then, as the two sat up in bed, straining their ears, there came from above them a gasping cry and the dull, soft thud of a falling body.

Beard sprang out of bed and rushed upstairs until his head came upon the level of the Youngmans' landing. He saw enough to send him shrieking down to Mr. Bevan upon the ground floor. "For God's sake, come here! There is murder!" he roared, fumbling with his shaking fingers at the handle of the landlord's bedroom.

His summons did not find the landlord entirely unprepared. That ill-boding thud had been loud enough to reach his ears. He sprang palpitating from his bed, and the two men, in their nightdresses, ascended the creaking staircase, their frightened faces lit up by the blaze of golden sunlight of a July morning.

Again they do not seem to have got farther than the point from which they could see the landing. That confused huddle of white-clad figures littered over the passage, with those glaring smears and blotches, were more than their nerves could stand. They could count three lying there, stark dead upon the landing. And there was someone moving in the bedroom. It was coming towards them. With horror-dilated eyes they saw William Godfrey Youngman framed in the open doorway, his white nightdress brilliant with ghastly streaks and the sleeve hanging torn over his hand.

"Mr. Beard," he cried, when he saw the two blood-less faces upon the stairs, "for God's sake fetch a surgeon! I believe there is some alive yet!" Then, as they turned and ran down stairs again, he called after them the singular explanation to which he ever after-wards adhered. "My mother has done all this," he cried; "she has murdered my two brothers and my sweetheart, and I in self-defence believe that I have murdered her."

The two men did not stop to discuss the question with him. They had both rushed to their rooms and huddled on some clothes. Then they ran out of the house in search of a surgeon and a policeman, leaving Youngman still standing on the stair repeating his strange explanation. How sweet the morning air must have seemed to them when they were once clear of the accursed house, and how the honest milkmen, with their swinging tins, must have stared at those two rushing and dishevelled figures. But they had not far to go. John Varney, of P Division, as solid and unimagi-native as the law which he represents, was standing at the street corner, and he came clumping back with reassuring slowness and dignity.

"Oh, policeman, here is a sight! What shall I do?" cried Youngman, as he saw the glazed official hat coming up the stair.

Constable Varney is not shaken by that horrid cluster of death. His advice is practical and to the point.

"Go and dress yourself!" said he.

"I struck my mother, but it was in self-defence," cried the other. "Would you not have done the same? It is the law."

Constable Varney is not to be drawn into giving a legal opinion, but he is quite convinced that the best thing for Youngman to do is to put on some clothes.

And now a crowd had begun to assemble in the street, and another policeman and an inspector had arrived. It was clear that, whether Youngman's story was correct or not, he was a self-confessed homicide, and that the law must hold her grip on him. But when a dagger-shaped knife, splintered by the force of repeated blows, was found upon the floor, and Youngman had to confess that it belonged to him; when also it was observed that ferocious strength and energy were needed to produce the wounds inflicted, it became increasingly evident that, instead of being a mere victim of circumstances, this man was one of the criminals of a century. But all evidence must be circumstantial, for mother, sweetheart, brothers—the mouths of all were closed in the one indiscriminate butchery.

The horror and the apparent purposelessness of the deed roused public excitement and indignation to the highest pitch. The miserable sum for which poor Mary was insured appeared to be the sole motive of the crime; the prisoner's eagerness to have the business concluded, and his desire to have the letters destroyed in which he had urged it, forming the strongest evidence against him. At the same time, his calm assumption that things would be arranged as he wished them to be, and that the Argus Insurance Office would pay over the money to one who was neither husband nor relative of the deceased, pointed to an ignorance of the ways of business or a belief in his own powers of managing, which in either case resembled insanity. When, in addition, it came out at the trial that the family was sodden with lunacy upon both sides, that the wife's mother and the husband's brother were in asylums, and that the husband's father had been in an asylum, but had become "tolerably sensible" before his death, it is doubtful whether the case should not have been judged upon medical rather than upon criminal grounds. In these more scientific and more humanitarian days, it is perhaps doubtful whether Youngman would have been hanged, but there was never any doubt as to his fate in 1860.

The trial came off at the Central Criminal Court upon August 16th, before Mr. Justice Williams. Few fresh details came out, save that the knife has been in the prisoner's possession for some time. He had exhibited it once in a bar, upon which a bystander, with the good British love of law and order, had remarked that that was not a fit knife for any man to carry.

"Anybody," said Youngman, in reply, "has the right to carry such a knife if he thinks proper in his own defence."

Perhaps the objector did not realize how near he may have been at that moment to getting its point between his ribs. Nothing serious against the prisoner's previous character came out at the trial, and he adhered steadfastly to his own account of the tragedy. In summing up, however, Justice Williams pointed out that, if the prisoner's story were true, it meant that he had disarmed his mother and got possession of the knife. What necessity was there, then, for him to kill her — and why should he deal her repeated wounds? This argument, and the fact that there were no stains upon the hands of the mother, prevailed with the jury, and sentence was duly passed upon the prisoner.

Youngman had shown an unmoved demeanour in the dock, but he gave signs of an irritable, and occasionally of a violent, temper in prison. His father visited him, and the prisoner burst instantly into fierce reproaches against his treatment of his family — reproaches for which there seem to have been no justification. Another thing which appeared to have galled him to the quick was the remark of the publican, which first reached his ears at the trial, to the effect that Mary had better hang herself in the skittle-yard than marry such a man. His self-esteem, the strongest trait in his nature, was cruelly wounded by such a speech.

"Only one thing I wish," he cried, furiously, "that I could get hold of this man Spicer, for I would strike his head off." The unnatural and bloodthirsty character of the threat is characteristic of the homicidal maniac. "Do you suppose," he added, with a fine touch of vanity, "that a man of my determination and spirit would have heard these words used in my presence without striking the man who used them to the ground?"

But in spite of exhortation and persuasion, he carried his secret with him to the grave. He never varied from the story which he had probably concocted before the event.

"Do not leave the world with a lie on your lips," said the chaplain, as they walked to the scaffold.

"Well, if I wanted to tell a lie, I would say that I did it," was his retort. He hoped to the end, with his serene self-belief, that the story which he had put forward could not fail eventually to be accepted. Even on the scaffold he was on the alert for a reprieve.

It was on the 4th of September, a little more than a month after the commission of his crime, that he was led out in front of Horsemonger Gaol to suffer his punishment. A concourse of 30,000 people, many of whom had waited all night, raised a brutal howl at his appearance. It was remarked at the time that it was one of the very few instances of capital punishment in which no sympathizer or philanthropist of any sort could be found to raise a single voice against the death penalty.

The man died quietly and coolly. "Thank you, Mr. Jessopp," said he to the chaplain, "for your great kindness. See my brother and take my love to him, and all at home."

And so, with the snick of a bolt and the jar of a rope, ended one of the most sanguinary, and also one of the most unaccountable, incidents in English criminal annals. That the man was guilty seems to admit no doubt, and yet it must be confessed that circumstantial evidence can never be absolutely convincing, and that it is only the critical student of such cases who realizes how often a damning chain of evidence may, by some slight change, be made to bear an entirely different interpretation.

The Love Affair of
George Vincent Parker

T HE STUDENT of criminal annals will find, upon classifying his cases, that the two causes which are the most likely to incite a human being to the crime of murder are the lust of money and the black resentment of disappointed love. Of these, the the latter are both rarer and more interesting, for they are subtler in their inception and deeper in their psychology. The mind can find no possible sympathy with the brutal greed and selfishness which weighs a purse against a life; but there is something more spiritual in the case of the man who is driven by jealousy and misery to a temporary madness of violence. To use the language of science, it is the passionate, as distinguished from the instinctive, criminal type. The two classes of crime may be punished by the same severity, but we feel that they are not equally sordid, and that none of us is capable of saying how he might act if his affections and his self-respect were suddenly and cruelly outraged. Even when we endorse the verdict, it is still possible to feel some shred of pity for the criminal. His offence has not been the result of a self-interested and cold-blooded plotting, but it has been the consequence — however monstrous and disproportionate — of a cause for which others were responsible. As an

example of such a crime, I would recite the circumstances connected with George Vincent Parker, making
some alteration in the names of persons and of places
wherever there is a possibility that pain might be
inflicted by their disclosure.

Nearly forty years ago, there lived in one of our
Midland cities a certain Mr. Parker, who did a considerable business as a commission agent. He was an
excellent man of affairs, and, during those progressive
years which intervened between the Crimean and the
American wars, his fortune increased rapidly. He built
himself a villa in a pleasant suburb outside the town,
and, being blessed with a charming and sympathetic
wife, there was every prospect that the evening of his
days would be spent in happiness. The only trouble
which he had to contend with was his inability to
understand the character of his only son, or to determine what plans he should make for his future.

George Vincent Parker, the young man in question,
was of a type which continually recurs and which verges
always upon the tragic. By some trick of atavism, he
had no love for the great city and its roaring life, none
for the weary round of business, and no ambition to
share the rewards which successful business brings. He
had no sympathy with his father's works or his father's
ways, and the life of the office was hateful to him. This
aversion to work could not, however, be ascribed to
viciousness or indolence. It was innate and constitutional. In other directions his mind was alert and
receptive. He loved music and showed a remarkable
aptitude for it. He was an excellent linguist and had
some taste in painting. In a word, he was a man of
artistic temperament, with all the failings of nerve and
of character which that temperament implies. In

London he would have met hundreds of the same type, and would have found a congenial occupation in making small incursions into literature and dabbling in criticism. Among the cotton-brokers of the Midlands, his position was at that time an isolated one, and his father could only shake his head and pronounce him to be quite unfit to carry on the family business. He was gentle in his disposition, reserved with strangers, but very popular among his few friends. Once or twice it had been remarked that he was capable of considerable bursts of passion when he thought himself ill-used.

This is a type of man for whom the practical workers of the world have no affection, but it is one which invariably appeals to the feminine nature. There is a certain helplessness about it, and a naïve appeal for sympathy, to which a woman's heart readily responds — and it is the strongest, most vigorous woman who is the first to answer the appeal. We do not know what other consolers this quiet dilettante may have found, but the details of one such connection have come down to us.

It was at a musical evening at the house of a local doctor that he first met Miss Mary Groves. The doctor was her uncle, and she had come to town to visit him, but her life was spent in attendance upon her grandfather, who was a very virile old gentleman, whose eighty years did not prevent him from fulfilling all those duties of a country gentleman, including those of the magisterial bench. After the quiet of a secluded manor house, the girl, in the first flush of her youth and her beauty, enjoyed the life of the town, and seems to have been particularly attracted by this refined young musician, whose appearance and manners suggested that touch of romance for which a young girl craves.

He on his side was drawn to her by her country fresh-
ness and by the sympathy which she showed for him.
Before she returned to the Manor House, friendship
had grown into love and the pair were engaged.

But the engagement was not looked upon with
much favour by either of the families concerned. Old
Parker had died, and his widow was left with sufficient
means to live in comfort, but it became more impera-
tive than ever that some profession should be found for
the son. His invincible repugnance to business still
stood in the way. On the other hand, the young lady
came of a good stock, and her relations, headed by the
old country squire, objected to her marriage with a
penniless young man of curious tastes and character.
So, for four years, the engagement dragged along,
during which the lovers corresponded continually, but
seldom met. At the end of that time, he was twenty-five
and she was twenty-three, but the prospect of their
union seemed as remote as ever.

At last, the prayers of her relatives overcame her
constancy, and she took steps to break the tie which
held them together. This she endeavoured to do by a
change in the tone of her letters, and by ominous
passages to prepare him for the coming blow.

On August 12th, 18—, she wrote that she had met a
clergyman who was the most delightful man she had
ever seen in her life. "He has been staying with us," she
said, "and grandfather thought that he would just suit
me, but that would not do." This passage, in spite of
the few lukewarm words of reassurance, disturbed
young Vincent Parker exceedingly. His mother testified
afterwards to the extreme depression into which he was
thrown, which was the less remarkable as he was a man

who suffered from constitutional low spirits, and who always took the darkest view upon every subject.

Another letter reached him next day which was more decided in its tone.

"I have a good deal to say to you, and it had better be said at once," said she. "My grandfather has found out about our correspondence, and is wild that there should be any obstacle to the match between the clergyman and me. I want you to release me that I may have it to say that I am free. Don't take this too hardly, in pity for me. I shall not marry if I can help it."

This second letter had an overpowering effect. His state was such that his mother had to ask a family friend to sit up with him all night. He paced up and down in an extreme state of nervous excitement, bursting constantly into tears. When he lay down, his hands and feet twitched convulsively. Morphia was administered, but without effect. He refused all food. He had the utmost difficulty in answering the letter, and, when he did so next day, it was with the help of the friend who had stayed with him all night. His answer was reasonable and also affectionate.

"My dearest Mary," he said. "Dearest you will always be to me. To say that I am not terribly cut up would be a lie, but at any rate you know that I am not the man to stand in your way. I answer nothing to your last letter except that I wish to hear from your own lips what your wishes are, and I will then accede to them. You know me too well to think that I would then give way to any unnecessary nonsense or sentimentalism. Before I leave England I wish to see you once again, and for the last time, though God knows what misery it gives me to say so. You will admit that my desire to see

you is but natural. Say in your next where you will
meet me. — Ever, dearest Mary, your affectionate
GEORGE."

Next day, he wrote another letter in which he again
implored her to give him an appointment, saying that
any place between their house and Standwell, the
nearest village, would do. "I am ill and thoroughly
upset, and I do not wonder that you are," said he. "We
shall both be happier and better in mind as well as in
body after this last interview. I shall be at your appointment, *coûte qu'il coûte.* — Always your affectionate
GEORGE."

There seems to have been an answer to this letter,
actually making an appointment, for he wrote again
upon Wednesday, the 19th. "My dear Mary," said he,
"I will only say here that I will arrive by the train you
mention and that I hope, dear Mary, that you will not
bother yourself unnecessarily about all this so far as I
am concerned. For my own peace of mind I wish to see
you, which I hope you won't think selfish. *Du reste* I only
repeat what I have already said. I have but to hear from
you what your wishes are and they shall be complied
with. I have sufficient *savoir faire* not to make a bother
about what cannot be helped. Don't let me be the cause
of any row between you and your grandpapa. If you
like to call at the inn I will not stir out until you come,
but I leave this to your judgment."

As Professor Owen would reconstruct an entire
animal out of a single bone, so from this one little letter
the man stands flagrantly revealed. The scraps of
French, the self-conscious allusion to his own *savoir
faire,* the florid assurances which mean nothing, they
are all so many strokes in a subtle self-portrait.

Miss Groves had already repented the appointment

which she had given him. There may have been some traits in this eccentric lover whom she had abandoned which recurred to her memory and warned her not to trust herself in his power. "My dear George," she wrote — and her letter must have crossed his last one — "I write this in the greatest haste to tell you not to come on any account. I leave here to-day, and can't tell when I can or shall be back. I do not wish to see you if it can possibly be avoided, and indeed there will be no chance now, so we had best end this state of suspense at once and say good-bye without seeing each other. I feel sure I could not stand the meeting. If you write once more within the next three days I shall get it, but not later than that time without its being seen, for my letters are strictly watched and even opened. — Yours truly, MARY."

This letter seems to have brought any vague schemes which may have been already forming in the young man's mind to an immediate head. If he had only three days in which he might see her, he could not afford to waste any time. On the same day, he went on to the country town, but, as it was late, he did not go on to Standwell, which was her station. The waiters at the Midland Hotel noticed his curious demeanour and his vacant eye. He wandered about the coffee-room, muttering to himself, and, although he ordered chops and tea, he swallowed nothing but some brandy and soda.

Next morning, August 21st, he took a ticket to Standwell and arrived there at half-past eleven. From Standwell Station to the Manor House at which Miss Groves resided with the old squire is two miles. There is an inn close to the station called "The Bull's Head." Vincent Parker called there and ordered some brandy.

He then asked whether a note had been left there for him, and seemed much disturbed upon hearing that there was none. Then, the time being about a quarter past twelve, he went off in the direction of the Manor House.

About two miles upon the other side of the Manor House, and four miles from the Bull's Head Inn, there is a thriving grammar school, the headmaster of which was a friend of the Groves family and had some slight acquaintance with Vincent Parker. The young man thought, therefore, that this would be the best place for him to apply for information, and he arrived at the school about half-past one. The headmaster was no doubt considerably astonished at the appearance of this dishevelled and brandy-smelling visitor, but he answered his questions with discretion and courtesy.

"I have called upon you," said Parker, "as a friend of Miss Groves. I suppose you know that there is an engagement between us?"

"I understood that there *was* an engagement, and that it had been broken off," said the master.

"Yes," Parker answered. "She has written to me to break off the engagement and declines to see me. I want to know how matters stand."

"Anything I may know," said the master, "is in confidence, and so I cannot tell you."

"I will find it out sooner or later," said Parker, and then asked who the clergyman was who had been staying at the Manor House. The master acknowledged that there had been one, but refused to give the name. Parker then asked whether Miss Groves was at the Manor House and if any coercion was being used to her. The other answered that she was at the Manor House and that no coercion was being used.

"Sooner or later I must see her," said Parker. "I have written to release her from her engagement, but I must hear from her own lips that she gives me up. She is of age and must please herself. I know that I am not a good match, and I do not wish to stand in her way."

The master then remarked that it was time for school, but that he should be free again at half-past four if Parker had anything more to say to him, and Parker left, promising to return. It is not known how he spent the next two hours, but he may have found some country inn in which he obtained some luncheon. At half-past four, he was back at the school, and asked the master for advice as to how to act. The master suggested that his best course was to write a note to Miss Groves and to make an appointment with her for next morning.

"If you were to call at the house, perhaps Miss Groves would see you," said this sympathetic and most injudicious master.

"I will do so and get it off my mind," said Vincent Parker.

It was about five o'clock when he left the school, his manner at that time being perfectly calm and collected.

It was forty minutes later when the discarded lover arrived at the house of his sweetheart. He knocked at the door and asked for Miss Groves. She had probably seen him as he came down the drive, for she met him at the drawing-room door as he came in, and she invited him to come with her into the garden. Her heart was in her mouth, no doubt, lest her grandfather should see him and a scene ensue. It was safer to have him in the garden than in the house. They walked out, therefore, and half an hour later they were seen chatting quietly upon one of the benches. A little afterwards, the maid went out and told Miss Groves that tea was ready. She came in alone, and it is suggestive of the views taken by the grandfather that there seems to have been no question about Parker coming in also to tea. She came out again into the garden and sat for a long time with the young man, after which they seem to have set off together for a stroll down the country lanes.

What passed during that walk, what recriminations upon his part, what retorts upon hers, will never now be known. They were only once seen in the course of it. At about half-past eight o'clock, a labourer, coming up a long lane which led from the high road to the Manor House, saw a man and a woman walking together. As he passed them, he recognized in the dusk that the lady was Miss Groves, the granddaughter of the squire. When he looked back, he saw that they had stopped and were standing face to face, conversing.

A very short time after this, Reuben Conway, a workman, was passing down this lane when he heard a low sound of moaning. He stood listening, and in the silence of the country evening he became aware that this ominous sound was drawing nearer to him. A wall flanked one side of the lane, and, as he stared about him, his eye caught something moving slowly down the black shadow at the side. For a moment, it must have seemed to him to be some wounded animal, but, as he approached it, he saw to his astonishment that it was a woman who was slowly stumbling along, guided and supporting herself by her hand against the wall. With a cry of horror, he found himself looking into the face of Miss Groves, glimmering white through the darkness.

"Take me home!" she whispered. "Take me home! The gentleman down there has been murdering me."

The horrified labourer put his arms round her, and carried her for about twenty yards towards home.

"Can you see anyone down the lane?" she asked, when he stopped for breath.

He looked, and through the dark tunnel of trees he saw a black figure moving slowly behind them. The labourer waited, still propping up the girl's head, until young Parker overtook them.

"Who has been murdering Miss Groves?" asked Reuben Conway.

"I have stabbed her," said Parker, with the utmost coolness.

"Well, then, you had best help me to carry her home," said the labourer. So down the dark lane moved that singular procession: the rustic and the lover, with the body of the dying girl between them.

"Poor Mary!" Parker muttered. "Poor Mary! You should not have proved false to me!"

When they got as far as the lodge gate, Parker suggested that Reuben Conway should run and get something which might staunch the bleeding. He went, leaving these tragic lovers together for the last time. When he returned, he found Parker holding something to her throat.

"Is she living?" he asked.

"She is," said Parker.

"Oh, take me home!" wailed the poor girl.

A little farther upon their dolorous journey, they met two farmers, who helped them.

"Who has done this?" asked one of them.

"He knows and I know," said Parker, gloomily. "I am the man who has done this, and I shall be hanged for it. I have done it, and there is no question about that at all."

These replies never seem to have brought insult or invective upon his head, for everyone appears to have been silenced by the overwhelming tragedy of the situation.

"I am dying!" gasped poor Mary, and they were the last words which she ever said.

Inside the hall gates they met the poor old squire running wildly up on some vague rumour of a disaster. The bearers stopped as they saw the white hair gleaming through the darkness.

"What is amiss?" he cried.

Parker said, calmly, "It is your granddaughter Mary murdered."

"Who did it?" shrieked the old man.

"I did it."

"Who are you?" he cried.

"My name is Vincent Parker."

"Why did you do it?"

"She has deceived me, and the woman who deceives me must die."

The calm concentration of his manner seems to have silenced all reproaches.

"I told her I would kill her," said he, as they all entered the house together. "She knew my temper."

The body was carried into the kitchen and laid upon the table. In the meantime, Parker had followed the bewildered and heart-broken old man into the drawing-room, and, holding out a handful of things, including his watch and some money, he asked him if he would take care of them. The squire angrily refused. He then took two bundles of her letters out of his pocket — all that was left of their miserable love story.

"Will you take care of these?" said he. "You may read them, burn them, do what you like with them. I don't wish them to be brought into court."

The grandfather took the letters, and they were duly burned.

And now the doctor and the policeman, the twin attendants upon violence, came hurrying down the avenue. Poor Mary was dead upon the kitchen table, with three great wounds upon her throat. How, with a severed carotid, she could have come so far or lived so long is one of the marvels of the case.

As to the policeman, he had no trouble in looking for his prisoner. As he entered the room, Parker walked towards him and said that he wished to give himself up for murdering a young lady. When asked if he were aware of the nature of the charge, he said, "Yes, quite so, and I will go with you quietly, only let me see her first."

"What have you done with the knife?" asked the policeman.

Parker produced it from his pocket, a very ordinary one with a clasp blade. It is remarkable that two other penknives were afterwards found upon him. They took him into the kitchen, and he looked at his victim.

"I am far happier now that I have done it than before, and I hope that she is," said he.

This is the record of the murder of Mary Groves by Vincent Parker, a crime characterized by all that inconsequence and grim artlessness which distinguish fact from fiction. In fiction we make people say and do what we should conceive them to be likely to say or do, but in fact they say and do what no one would ever conceive to be likely. That those letters should be a prelude to murder, or that after a murder the criminal should endeavour to staunch the wounds of his victim, or hold such a conversation as that described with the old squire is what no human invention would hazard. One finds it very difficult, on reading all the letters and weighing the facts, to suppose that Vincent Parker came out that day with the preformed intention of killing his former sweetheart. But whether the dreadful idea was always there, or whether it came in some mad flash of passion provoked by their conversation, is what we shall never know. It is certain that she could not have seen anything dangerous in him up to the very instant of the crime, or she would certainly have appealed to the labourer who passed them in the lane.

The case, which excited the utmost interest through the length and breadth of England, was tried before Baron Martin at the next Assizes. There was no need to prove the guilt of the prisoner, since he openly gloried in it, but the whole question turned upon his sanity, and led to some curious complications which have caused the whole law upon the point to be reformed.

His relations were called to show that madness was rampant in the family, and that, out of ten cousins, five were insane. His mother appeared in the witness-box, contending with dreadful vehemence that her son was mad, and that her own marriage had been objected to on the ground of the madness latent in her blood. All the witnesses agreed that the prisoner was not an ill-tempered man, but sensitive, gentle, and accomplished, with a tendency to melancholy. The prison chaplain affirmed that he had held conversations with Parker, and that his moral perception seemed to be so entirely wanting that he hardly knew right from wrong. Two specialists in lunacy examined him, and said that they were of opinion that he was of unsound mind. The opinion was based upon the fact that the prisoner declared that he could not see that he had done any wrong.

"Miss Groves was promised to me," said he, "and therefore she was mine. I could do what I liked with her. Nothing short of a miracle will alter my convictions."

The doctor attempted to argue with him. "Suppose anyone took a picture from you, what steps would you take to recover it?" he asked.

"I should demand restitution," said he; "if not, I should take the thief's life without compunction."

The doctor pointed out that the law was there to be appealed to, but Parker answered that he had been born into the world without being consulted, and therefore he recognized the right of no man to judge him. The doctor's conclusion was that his moral sense was more vitiated than any case that he had seen. That this constitutes madness would, however, be a dangerous doctrine to urge, since it means that if a man were only wicked enough he would be screened from the punishment of his wickedness.

Baron Martin summed up in a commonsense manner. He declared that the world was full of eccentric people, and that to grant them all the immunity of madness would be a public danger. To be mad within the meaning of the law, a criminal should be in such a state as not to know that he has committed crime or incurred punishment. Now, it was clear that Parker did know this, since he had talked of being hanged. The Baron accordingly accepted the jury's finding of "Guilty," and sentenced the prisoner to death.

There the matter might very well have ended were it not for Baron Martin's conscientious scruples. His own ruling had been admirable, but the testimony of the mad doctors weighed heavily upon him, and his conscience was uneasy at the mere possibility that a man who was really not answerable for his actions should lose his life through his decision. It is probable that the thought kept him awake that night, for next morning he wrote to the Secretary of State, and told him that he shrank from the decision of such a case.

The Secretary of State, having carefully read the evidence and the judge's remarks, was about to confirm the decision of the latter, when, upon the very eve of the execution, there came a report from the gaol visitors — perfectly untrained observers — that Parker was showing undoubted signs of madness. This being so, the Secretary of State had no choice but to postpone the execution, and to appoint a commission of four eminent alienists to report upon the condition of the prisoner. These four reported unanimously that he was perfectly sane. It is an unwritten law, however, that a prisoner once reprieved is never executed, so Vincent Parker's sentence was commuted to penal servitude for life — a decision which satisfied, upon the whole, the conscience of the public.

The Debatable Case of
Mrs. Emsley

IN the fierce popular indignation which is excited by a sanguinary crime, there is a tendency, in which judges and juries share, to brush aside or to treat as irrelevant those doubts the benefit of which is supposed to be one of the privileges of the accused. Lord Tenterden has whittled down the theory of doubt by declaring that a jury is justified in giving its verdict upon such evidence as it would accept to be final in any of the issues of life. But when one looks back and remembers how often one has been very sure and yet has erred in the issues of life, how often what has seemed certain has failed us, and that which appeared impossible has come to pass, we feel that, if the criminal law has been conducted upon such principles, it is probably itself the giant murderer of England. Far wiser is the contention that it is better that ninety-nine guilty should escape than that one innocent man should suffer, and that, therefore, if it can be claimed that there is one chance in a hundred in favour of the prisoner, he is entitled to his acquittal. It cannot be doubted that if the Scotch verdict of "Not Proven," which neither condemns nor acquits, had been permissible in England, it would have been the outcome of many a case which, under our sterner law,

has ended upon the scaffold. Such a verdict would, I
fancy, have been hailed as a welcome compromise by
the judge and the jury who investigated the singular
circumstances which attended the case of Mrs. Mary
Emsley.

The stranger in London who wanders away from
the beaten paths and strays into the quarters in which
the workers dwell is astounded by their widespread
monotony, by the endless rows of uniform brick houses
broken only by the corner public-houses and more
infrequent chapels which are scattered amongst them.
The expansion of the great city has been largely caused
by the covering of district after district with these long
lines of humble dwellings, and the years between the
end of the Crimean War and 1860 saw great activity in
this direction. Many small builders, by continually
mortgaging what they had done, and using the capital
thus acquired to start fresh works which were themselves in turn mortgaged, contrived to erect street after
street, and eventually, on account of the general rise of
property, to make considerable fortunes. Amongst
these astute speculators there was one John Emsley,
who, dying, left his numerous houses and various
interests to his widow Mary.

Mary Emsley, now an old woman, had lived too
long in a humble fashion to change her way of life. She
was childless, and all the activities of her nature were
centred upon the economical management of her
property, and the collection of the weekly rents from
the humble tenants who occupied them. A grim, stern,
eccentric woman, she was an object of mingled dislike
and curiosity among the inhabitants of Grove Road,
Stepney, in which her house was situated. Her posses-
sions extended over Stratford, Bow, and Bethnal

Green, and in spite of her age she made long journeys, collecting, evicting, and managing, always showing a great capacity for the driving of a hard bargain. One of her small economies was that, when she needed help in managing these widespread properties, she preferred to employ irregular agents to engaging a salaried representative. There were many who did odd jobs for her, and among them were two men whose names were destined to become familiar to the public. The one was John Emms, a cobbler; the other George Mullins, a plasterer.

Mary Emsley, in spite of her wealth, lived entirely alone, save that on Saturdays a charwoman called to clean up the house. She showed also that extreme timidity and caution which are often characteristic of those who afterwards perish by violence — as if there lies in human nature some vague, instinctive power of prophecy. It was with reluctance that she ever opened her door, and each visitor who approached her was reconnoitred from the window of her area. Her fortune would have permitted her to indulge herself with every luxury, but the house was a small one, consisting of two stories and a basement, with a neglected back garden, and her mode of life was even simpler than her dwelling. It was a singular and most unnatural old age.

Mrs. Emsley was last seen alive upon the evening of Monday, August 13th, 1860. Upon that date, at seven o'clock, two neighbours perceived her sitting at her bedroom window. Next morning, shortly after ten, one of her irregular retainers called upon some matter of brass taps, but was unable to get any answer to his repeated knockings. During that Tuesday, many visitors had the same experience, and the Wednesday and Thursday passed without any sign of life within the

house. One would have thought that this would have
aroused instant suspicions, but the neighbours were so
accustomed to the widow's eccentricities that they were
slow to be alarmed. It was only upon the Friday, when
John Emms, the cobbler, found the same sinister
silence prevailing in the house, that a fear of foul play
came suddenly upon him. He ran round to Mr. Rose,
her attorney, and Mr. Faith, who was a distant relation,
and the three men returned to the house. On their way,
they picked up Police-constable Dillon, who accompanied them.

The front door was fastened and the windows
snibbed, so the party made their way over the garden
wall and so reached the back entrance, which they seem
to have opened without difficulty. John Emms led the
way, for he was intimately acquainted with the house.
On the ground floor there was no sign of the old
woman. The creak of their boots and the subdued
whisper of their voices were the only sounds which
broke the silence. They ascended the stair with a feeling
of reassurance. Perhaps it was all right after all. It was
quite probable that the eccentric widow might have
gone on a visit. And then, as they came upon the
landing, John Emms stood staring, and the others,
peering past him, saw that which struck the hope from
their hearts.

It was the footprint of a man, dimly outlined in
blood upon the wooden floor. The door of the front
room was nearly closed, and this dreadful portent lay in
front of it with the toes pointing away. The police-
constable pushed at the door, but something which lay
behind it prevented it from opening. At last, by their
united efforts, they effected an entrance. There lay the
unfortunate old woman, her lank limbs all asprawl

upon the floor, with two rolls of wall-paper under her arm and several others scattered in front of her. It was evident that the frightful blows which had crushed in her head had fallen upon her unforeseen, and had struck her senseless in an instant. She had none of that anticipation which is the only horror of death.

The news of the murder of so well-known an inhabitant caused the utmost excitement in the neighbourhood, and every effort was made to detect the assassin. A Government reward of £100 was soon raised to £300, but without avail. A careful examination of the house failed to reveal anything which might serve as a reliable clue. It was difficult to determine the hour of the murder, for there was reason to think that the dead woman occasionally neglected to make her bed, so that the fact that the bed was unmade did not prove that it had been slept in. She was fully dressed, as she would be in the evening, and it was unlikely that she would be doing business with wall-papers in the early morning. On the whole, then, the evidence seemed to point to the crime having been committed upon the Monday evening some time after seven. There had been no forcing of doors or windows, and therefore the murderer had been admitted by Mrs. Emsley. It was not consistent with her habits that she should admit anyone whom she did not know at such an hour, and the presence of the wall-papers showed that it was someone with whom she had business to transact. So far the police could hardly go wrong. The murderer appeared to have gained little by his crime, for the only money in the house, £48, was found concealed in the cellar, and nothing was missing save a few articles of no value. For weeks, the public waited impatiently for an arrest, and for weeks the police remained silent though not inactive.

Then an arrest was at last effected, and in a curiously dramatic fashion.

Amongst the numerous people who made small sums of money by helping the murdered woman, there was one respectable-looking man, named George Mullins — rather over fifty years of age, with the straight back of a man who has at some period been well drilled. As a matter of fact, he had served in the Irish Constabulary, and had undergone many other curious experiences before he had settled down as a plasterer in the East End of London. This man it was who called upon Sergeant Tanner, of the police, and laid before him a statement which promised to solve the whole mystery.

According to this account, Mullins had from the first been suspicious of Emms, the cobbler, and had taken steps to verify his suspicions, impelled partly by his love of justice and even more by his hope of the reward. The £300 bulked largely before his eyes. "If this only goes right, I'll take care of you," said he, on his first interview with the police, and added, in allusion to his own former connection with the force, that he "was clever at these matters." So clever was he that his account of what he had seen and done gave the police an excellent clue upon which to act.

It appears that the cobbler dwelt in a small cottage at the edge of an old brickfield. On this brickfield, and about fifty yards from the cottage, there stood a crumbling outhouse which had been abandoned. Mullins, it seems, had for some time back been keeping a watchful eye upon Emms, and he had observed him carrying a paper parcel from his cottage and concealing it somewhere in the shed. "Very likely," said the astute Mullins, "he is concealing some of the plunder which he has stolen." To the police, also, the theory seemed not impossible, and so, on the following morning, three of them, with Mullins hanging at their heels, appeared at Emms's cottage, and searched both it and the shed. Their efforts, however, were in vain, and nothing was found.

This result was by no means satisfactory to the observant Mullins, who rated them soundly for not having half-searched the shed, and persuaded them to try again. They did so under his supervision, and this time with the best results. Behind a slab in the outhouse they came on a paper parcel of a very curious nature. It was tied up with coarse tape, and, when opened, disclosed another parcel tied with waxed string. Within were found three small spoons and one large one, two lenses, and a cheque drawn in favour of Mrs. Emsley, and known to have been paid to her upon the day of the murder. There was no doubt that the other articles had also belonged to the dead woman. The discovery was of the first importance, then, and the whole party set off for the police-station, Emms covered with confusion and dismay, while Mullins swelled with all the pride of the successful amateur detective. But his triumph did not last long. At the police-station, the inspector charged him with being himself concerned in the death of Mrs. Emsley.

"Is this the way that I am treated after giving you information?" he cried.

"If you are innocent no harm will befall you," said the inspector, and he was duly committed for trial.

This dramatic turning of the tables caused the deepest public excitement, and the utmost abhorrence was everywhere expressed against the man who was charged, not only with a very cold-blooded murder, but with a deliberate attempt to saddle another man with the guilt in the hope of receiving the reward. It was very soon seen that Emms at least was innocent, as he could prove the most convincing *alibi*. But if Emms was innocent, who was guilty, save the man who had placed the stolen articles in the outhouse — and who could this be save Mullins, who had informed the police that they were there? The case was prejudged by the public before ever the prisoner had appeared in the dock, and the evidence which the police had prepared against him was not such as to cause them to change their opinion. A damning series of facts were arraigned in proof of their theory of the case, and they were laid before the jury by Serjeant Parry at the Central Criminal Court upon the 25th of October, about ten weeks after the murder.

At first sight, the case against Mullins appeared to be irresistible. An examination of his rooms immediately after his arrest enabled the police to discover some tape upon his mantelpiece which corresponded very closely with the tape with which the parcel had been secured. There were thirty-two strands in each. There was also found a piece of cobbler's wax, such as would be needed to wax the string of the inner parcel. Cobbler's wax was not a substance which Mullins needed in his business, so that the theory of the prosecution was that he had simply procured it in order to throw suspicion upon the unfortunate cobbler. A plasterer's hammer, which might have inflicted the injuries, was also discovered upon the premises, and so was a spoon which corresponded closely to the spoons which Mrs. Emsley had lost. It was shown also that Mrs. Mullins had recently sold a small gold pencil-case to a neighbouring barman, and two witnesses were found to swear that this pencil-case belonged to Mrs.

Emsley and had been in her possession a short time before her death. There was also discovered a pair of boots, one of which appeared to fit the impression upon the floor, and medical evidence attested that there was some human hair upon the sole. The same medical evidence swore to a blood mark upon the gold pencil which had been sold by Mrs. Mullins. It was proved by the charwoman, who came upon Saturdays, that when she had been in the house two days before the murder, Mullins had called, bringing with him some rolls of wall-paper, and that he had been directed by Mrs. Emsley to carry it up to the room in which the tragedy afterwards occurred. Now, it was clear that Mrs. Emsley had been discussing wall-papers at the time that she was struck down, and what more natural than that it should have been with the person who had originally brought them? Again, it had been shown that during the day Mrs. Emsley had handed to Mullins a certain key. This key was found lying in the same room as the dead body, and the prosecution asked how it could have come there if Mullins did not bring it.

So far, the police had undoubtedly a very strong case, and they endeavoured to make it more convincing still by producing evidence to show that Mullins had been seen both going to the crime and coming away from it. One Raymond was ready to swear that at eight o'clock that evening he had caught a glimpse of him in the street near Mrs. Emsley's. He was wearing a black billycock hat. A sailor was produced who testified that he had seen him at Stepney Green a little after five next morning. According to the sailor's account, his attention was attracted by the nervous manner and excited appearance of the man whom he had met, and also by the fact that his pockets were very bulging. He was wearing a brown hat. When he heard of the murder, he had of his own accord given information to the police, and he would swear that Mullins was the man whom he had seen.

This was the case as presented against the accused, and it was fortified by many smaller points of suspicion. One of them was that, when he was giving the police information about Emms, he had remarked that Emms was about the only man to whom Mrs. Emsley would open her door.

"Wouldn't she open it for you, Mullins?" asked the policeman.

"No," said he. "She would have called to me from the window of the area."

This answer of his—which was shown to be untrue—told very heavily against him at the trial.

It was a grave task which Mr. Best had to perform when he rose to answer this complicated and widely-reaching indictment. He first of all endeavoured to establish an *alibi* by calling Mullins's children, who were ready to testify that he came home particularly early upon that particular Monday. Their evidence, however, was not very conclusive, and was shaken by the laundress, who showed that they were confusing one day with another. As regards the boot, the counsel pointed out that human hair was used by plasterers in their work, and he commented upon the failure of the prosecution to prove that there was blood upon the very boot which was supposed to have produced the blood-print. He also showed, as regards the bloodstain upon the pencil-case, that the barman upon buying the pencil had carefully cleaned and polished it, so that, if there was any blood upon it, it was certainly not that of Mrs. Emsley. He also commented upon the discrepancy of the evidence between Raymond, who saw the accused at eight in the evening in a black hat, and the sailor, who met him at five in the morning in a brown one. If the theory of the prosecution was that the accused had spent the night in the house of the murdered woman, how came his hat to be changed? One or other or both the witnesses must be worthless. Besides, the sailor had met his mysterious stranger at Stepney Green, which was quite out of the line between the scene of the crime and Mullins's lodgings. As to the bulging pockets, only a few small articles had been taken from the house, and they would certainly not cause the robber's pockets to bulge. There was no evidence either from Raymond or from the sailor that the prisoner was carrying the plasterer's hammer with which the deed was supposed to have been done.

And now he produced two new and very important witnesses, whose evidence furnished another of those sudden surprises with which the case had abounded. Mrs. Barnes, who lived in Grove Road, opposite to the scene of the murder, was prepared to swear that at twenty minutes to ten on Tuesday morning—twelve hours after the time of the commission of the crime according to the police theory—she saw someone moving paper-hangings in the top room, and that she also saw the right-hand window open a little way. Now, in either of these points she might be the victim of a delusion, but it is difficult to think that she was mistaken in them both. If there was really someone in the room at that hour, whether it was Mrs. Emsley or her assassin, in either case it proved the theory of the prosecution to be entirely mistaken.

The second piece of evidence was from Stephenson, a builder, who testified that, upon that Tuesday morning, he had seen one Rowland, also a builder, come out of some house with wall-papers in his hand. This was a little after ten o'clock. He could not swear to the house, but he thought that it was Mrs. Emsley's. Rowland was hurrying past him when he stopped him and asked him — they were acquaintances — whether he was in the paper line.

"Yes; didn't you know that?" said Rowland.

"No," said Stephenson, "else I should have given you a job or two."

"Oh, yes, I was bred up to it," said Rowland, and went on his way.

In answer to this, Rowland appeared in the box and stated that he considered Stephenson to be half-witted. He acknowledged the meeting and the conversation, but asserted that it was several days before. As a matter of fact, he was engaged in papering the house next to Mrs. Emsley's, and it was from that that he had emerged.

So stood the issues when the Chief Baron entered upon the difficult task of summing up. Some of the evidence upon which the police had principally relied was brushed aside by him very lightly. As to the tape, most tape consisted of thirty-two strands, and it appeared to him that the two pieces were not exactly of one sort. Cobbler's wax was not an uncommon substance, and a plasterer could not be blamed for possessing a plasterer's hammer. The boot, too, was not so exactly like the blood-print that any conclusions could be drawn from it. The weak point of the defence was that it was almost certain that Mullins hid the things in the shed. If he did not commit the crime, why did he not volunteer a statement as to how the things came into his possession? His remark that Mrs. Emsley would not open the door to him, when it was certain that she would do so, was very much against him. On the other hand, the conflicting evidence of the sailor and of the other man who had seen Mullins near the scene of the crime was not very convincing, nor did he consider the incident of the key to be at all conclusive, since the key might have been returned in the course of the day. On the whole, everything might be got round except the hiding of the parcel in the shed, and that was so exceedingly damning that, even without anything else, it amounted to a formidable case.

The jury deliberated for three hours and then brought in a verdict of "Guilty," in which the judge concurred. Some of his words, however, in passing sentence, were such as to show that his mind was by no means convinced upon the point.

"If you can even now make it manifest that you are innocent of the charge," said he, "I do not doubt that every attention will be paid to any cogent proof laid before those with whom it rests to carry out the finding of the law."

To allude to the possibility of a man's innocence and at the same time to condemn him to be hanged strikes the lay mind as being a rather barbarous and illogical proceeding. It is true that the cumulative force of the evidence against Mullins was very strong, and that investigation proved the man's antecedents to have been of the worst. But still, circumstantial evidence, even when it all points one way and there is nothing to be urged upon the other side, cannot be received with too great caution, for it is nearly always possible to twist it to some other meaning.

In this case, even allowing that the evidence for an *alibi* furnished by Mullins's children was worthless, and allowing also that Mr. Stephenson's evidence may be set aside, there remains the positive and absolutely disinterested testimony of Mrs. Barnes, which would seem to show that, even if Mullins did the crime, he did it in an entirely different way to that which the police imagined. Besides, is it not on the face of it most improbable that a man should commit a murder at eight o'clock or so in the evening, should remain all night in the house with the body of his victim, that he should do this in the dark — for a light moving about the house would have been certainly remarked by the neighbours — that he should not escape during the darkness, but that he should wait for the full sunlight of an August morning before he emerged?

After reading the evidence one is left with an irresistible impression that, though Mullins was very likely guilty, the police were never able to establish the details of the crime, and that there was a risk of a miscarriage of justice when the death sentence was carried out.

There was much discussion among the legal profession at the time as to the sufficiency of the evidence, but the general public was quite satisfied, for the crime was such a shocking one that universal prejudice was excited against the accused. Mullins was hanged on the 19th of November, and he left a statement behind him reaffirming his own innocence. He never attempted to explain the circumstances which cost him his life, but he declared in his last hours that he believed Emms to be innocent of the murder, which some have taken to be a confession that he had himself placed the incriminating articles in the shed. Forty years have served to throw no fresh light upon the matter.

EDITOR'S NOTE

The *"Strange Studies from Life"* were not Sir Arthur Conan Doyle's first ventures into the study of true crime. Twice before, he had written on the subject. *"The Bravoes of Market-Drayton,"* appearing in CHAMBERS'S JOURNAL of August 1889, is a recounting of an 1828 case he probably first heard of when serving as an unpaid medical assistant to the cantankerous Dr. Elliot, of Ruyton in Shropshire, in the summer of 1878. Nothing at all is known at this time of his sources for "The Voyage of the 'Flowery Land'" (to use its manuscript title), which was published in the Louisville COURIER-JOURNAL for March 19, 1899 and in other U.S. newspapers at about the same time under a variety of headline titles (although the 1863 mutiny had received extensive newspaper attention when it occurred). These pieces, as well as the more conventional "The Duello in France," from the CORNHILL magazine of December 1890, follow.

One might argue that, to these works, ought to be added Sir Arthur's writings in defense of George Edalji (1907) and Oscar Slater (1912), two men wrongly convicted of crime, both of whom were eventually vindicated largely owing to Doyle's efforts. These pamphlets, articles, and letters to the press, however, were polemic in nature rather than narrative, and both cases have been the subjects of books of their own. For these reasons, we have deemed them inappropriate for this volume.

47

Nor did Sir Arthur's interest in crime flag in later life. In 1911, he purchased the crime library of the late Sir William S. Gilbert, of Gilbert and Sullivan fame, whose hobby had been the examination of true criminal cases. Merging his knowledge of the history of crime with his newly professed Spiritualist beliefs, Doyle published "A New Light on Old Crimes" in the STRAND magazine for January 1920, collecting it in the posthumous THE EDGE OF THE UNKNOWN (1930). "A New Light on Old Crimes" is of considerable interest whether or not one credits Spiritualism, and it is presented here, in a slightly abridged form, to make this volume of Conan Doyle's true crime writings complete.

The Bravoes of
Market-Drayton

To the north of the Wrekin, amid the rolling pastoral country which forms the borders of the counties of Shropshire and Staffordshire, there lies as fair a stretch of rustic England as could be found in the length and breadth of the land. Away to the south-east lie the great Staffordshire potteries; and farther south still, a long dusky pall marks the region of coal and iron. On the banks of the Torn, however, there are sprinkled pretty country villages, and sleepy market towns which have altered little during the last hundred years, save that the mosses have grown longer, and the red bricks have faded into a more mellow tint. The traveller who in the days of our grandfathers was whirled through this beautiful region upon the box-seat of the Liverpool and Shrewsbury coach, was deeply impressed by the Arcadian simplicity of the peasants, and congratulated himself that innocence, long pushed out of the great cities, could still find a refuge amid these peaceful scenes. Most likely he would have smiled incredulously had he been informed that neither in the dens of Whitechapel nor in the slums of Birmingham was morality so lax or human life so cheap as in the fair region which he was admiring.

How such a state of things came about it is difficult

now to determine. It may be that the very quiet and beauty of the place caused those precautions and safeguards to be relaxed which may nip crime in the bud. Sir Robert Peel's new police had not yet been established. Even in London the inefficient "Charley" still reigned supreme, and was only replaced by the more efficient Bow Street "runner" after the crime had been committed. It may be imagined, therefore, that among the cider orchards and sheep-walks of Shropshire the arm of Justice, however powerful to revenge, could do little to protect. No doubt, small offences undetected had led to larger ones, and those to larger still, until, in the year 1828, a large portion of the peasant population were banded together to defeat the law and to screen each other from the consequence of their misdeeds. This secret society might have succeeded in its object, had it not been for the unparalleled and most unnatural villainy of one of its members, whose absolutely callous and selfish conduct throws into the shade even the cold-blooded cruelty of his companions.

In the year 1827 a fine-looking young peasant named Thomas Ellson, in the prime of his manhood, was arrested at Market-Drayton upon two charges — the one of stealing potatoes, and the other of sheep-lifting, which in those days was still a hanging matter. The case for the prosecution broke down at the last moment on account of the inexplicable absence of an important witness named James Harrison. The crier of the court having three times summoned the absentee without any response, the charge was dismissed, and Thomas Ellson discharged with a caution. A louder crier still would have been needed to arouse James Harrison, for he was lying at that moment foully murdered in a hastily scooped grave within a mile of the court-house.

It appears that the gang which infested the country had, amidst their countless vices, one questionable virtue in their grim fidelity to each other. No red Macgregor attempting to free a clansman from the grasp of the Sassenach could have shown a more staunch and unscrupulous allegiance. The feeling was increased by the fact that the members of the league were generally connected with one another either by birth or marriage. When it became evident that Ellson's deliverance could only be wrought by the silencing of James Harrison, there appears to have been no hesitation as to the course to be followed.

The prime movers in the business were Ann Harris, who was the mother of Ellson by a former husband; and John Cox, his father-in-law. The latter was a fierce and turbulent old man, with two grown-up sons as savage as himself; while Mrs. Harris is described as being a ruddy-faced pleasant country woman, remarkable only for the brightness of her eyes. This pair of worthies having put their heads together, decided that James Harrison should be poisoned and that arsenic should be the drug. They applied, therefore, at several chemists', but without success. It is a remarkable commentary upon the general morality of Market-Drayton at this period that on applying at the local shop and being asked why she wanted the arsenic, Mrs. Harris ingenuously answered that it was simply "to poison that scoundrel, James Harrison." The drug was refused; but the speech appears to have been passed by as a very ordinary one, for no steps were taken to inform the authorities or to warn the threatened man.

Being unable to effect their purpose in this manner, the mother and the father-in-law determined to resort to violence. Being old and feeble themselves, they resolved to hire assassins for the job, which appears to have been neither a difficult nor an expensive matter in those regions. For five pounds, three stout young men were procured who were prepared to deal in human lives as readily as any Italian bravo who ever handled a stiletto. Two of these were the sons of old Cox, John and Robert. The third was a young fellow named Pugh, who lodged in the same house as the proposed victim. The spectacle of three smock-frocked English yokels selling themselves at thirty-three shillings and fourpence a head to murder a man against whom they had no personal grudge is one which is happily unique in the annals of crime.

The men earned their blood-money. On the next evening, Pugh proposed to the unsuspecting Harrison that they should slip out together and steal bacon, an invitation which appears to have had a fatal seduction to the Draytonian of the period. Harrison accompanied him upon the expedition, and presently, in a lonely corner, they came upon the two Coxes. One of them was digging in the ditch. Harrison expressed some curiosity as to what work he could have on hand at that time of night. He little dreamed that it was his own grave upon which he was looking. Presently, Pugh seized him by the throat, John Cox tripped up his heels, and together they strangled him. They bundled the body into the hole, covered it carefully up, and calmly returned to their beds. Next morning, as already recorded, the court crier cried in vain, and Thomas Ellson became a free man once more.

Upon his liberation, his associates naturally enough

explained to him with some exultation the means which they had adopted to silence the witness for the prosecution. The young Coxes, Pugh, and his mother all told him the same story. The unfortunate Mrs. Harris had already found occasion to regret the steps which she had taken, for Pugh, who appears to have been a most hardened young scoundrel, had already begun to extort money out of her on the strength of his knowledge. Robert Cox, too, had remarked to her with an oath: "If thee doesn't give me more money, I will fetch him and rear him up against thy door." The rustic villains seem to have seen their way to unlimited beer by working upon the feelings of the old country woman.

One would think that the lowest depths of human infamy had been already plumbed in this matter; but it remained for Thomas Ellson, the rescued man, to cap all the iniquities of his companions. About a year after his release, he was apprehended upon a charge of fowl-stealing, and in order to escape the trifling punishment allotted to that offence, he instantly told the whole story of the doing away with James Harrison. Had his confession come from horror at their crime, it might have been laudable; but the whole circumstances of the case showed that it was merely a cold-blooded bid for the remission of a small sentence at the cost of the lives of his own mother and his associates. Deep as their guilt was, it had at least been incurred in order to save this heartless villain from the fate which he had well deserved.

The trial which ensued excited the utmost interest in all parts of England. Ann Harris, John Cox, John Cox the younger, Robert Cox, and James Pugh were all arraigned for the murder of James Harrison. The wretched remnant of mortality had been dug up from the ditch, and could only be recognized by the clothes and by the colour of the hair. The whole case against the accused rested upon the very flimsiest evidence, save for Thomas Ellson's statement, which was delivered with a clearness and precision which no cross-examination could shake. He recounted the various conversations in which the different prisoners, including his mother, had admitted their guilt, as calmly and as imperturbably as though there were nothing at stake upon it. From the time when Pugh " 'ticed un out o' feyther's house to steal some bacon," to the final tragedy, when he "gripped un by the throat," every detail came out in its due order. He met his mother's gaze steadily as he swore that she had confided to him that she had contributed fifty shillings towards the removing of the witness. No more repulsive spectacle has ever been witnessed in an English court of justice than this cold-blooded villain calmly swearing away the life of the woman who bore him, whose crime had arisen from her extravagant affection for him, and all to save himself from a temporary inconvenience.

Mr. Phillips, the counsel for the defence, did all that he could to shake Ellson's evidence; but though he aroused the loathing of the whole court by the skilful way in which he brought out the scoundrel's motives and character, he was unable to shake him as to his facts. A verdict of guilty was returned against the whole band, and sentence of death duly passed upon them.

On the 4th of July 1828 the awful punishment was actually carried out upon Pugh and the younger Cox, the two who had laid hands upon the deceased. Pugh declared that death was a relief to him, as Harrison was always, night and day, by his side. Cox, on the other hand, died sullenly, without any sign of repentance for the terrible crime for which his life was forfeited. Thomas Ellson was compelled to be present at the execution, as a warning to him to discontinue his evil practices.

Mrs. Harris and the elder Cox were carried across the seas, and passed the short remainder of their lives in the dreary convict barracks which stood upon the site of what is now the beautiful town of Sydney. The air of the Shropshire downs was the sweeter for the dispersal of the precious band; and it is on record that this salutary example brought it home to the rustics that the law was still a power in the land, and that, looking upon it as a mere commercial transaction, the trade of the bravo was not one which could flourish upon English soil.

The Voyage of the "Flowery Land"

A STEAM TUG was puffing wheezily in front of the high-masted, barque-rigged clipper. With her fresh-painted, glistening black sides, her sharp sloping bows, and her cutaway counter, she was the very picture of a fast, well-found ocean-going sailing ship, but those who knew anything about her may have made her the text of a sermon as to how the British seaman was being elbowed out of existence. In this respect she was the scandal of the river. Chinamen, French, Norwegians, Spaniards, Turks — she carried an epitome of the human race. They were working hard cleaning up the decks and fastening down the hatches, but the big burly mate tore his hair when he found that hardly a man on board could understand an order in English.

Capt. John Smith had taken his younger brother, George Smith, as a passenger and companion for the voyage, in the hope that it might be beneficial to his health. They were seated now at each side of the round table, an open bottle of champagne between them, when the mate came in answer to a summons, his eyes still smouldering after his recent outbursts.

"Well, Mr. Karswell," said the captain, "we have a long six months before us, I dare say, before we raise the light of Singapore. I thought you might like to join us in a glass to our better acquaintance and to a lucky voyage."

He was a jovial, genial soul, this captain, with good humour shining from his red, weather-stained face. The mate's gruffness relaxed before his kindly words, and he tossed off the glass of champagne which the other had filled for him.

"How does the ship strike you, Mr. Karswell?" asked the captain.

"There's nothing the matter with the ship, sir."

"Nor with the cargo, either," said the captain. "Champagne we are carrying — a hundred dozen cases. These and bales of cloth are our main lading. How about the crew, Mr. Karswell?"

The mate shook his head.

"They'll need thrashing into shape, and that's a fact, sir. I've been hustling and driving ever since we left the Pool. Why, except ourselves here and Taffir, the second mate, there's hardly an Englishman aboard. The steward, the cook, and the boy are Chinese, as I understand. Anderson, the carpenter, is a Norwegian. There's Early, the lad, he's English. Then there's one Frenchman, one Finn, one Turk, one Spaniard, one Greek, and one Negro, and as to the rest I don't know what they are, for I never saw the match of them before."

"They are from the Philippine Islands, half Spanish, half Malay," the captain answered. "We call them Manila men, for that's the port they all hail from. You'll find them good enough seamen, Mr. Karswell. I'll answer for it that they work well."

"I'll answer for it, too," said the big mate, with an ominous clenching of his great red fist.

Karswell was hard put to it to establish any order amongst the strange material with which he had to work. Taffir, the second mate, was a mild young man, a good seaman and a pleasant companion, but hardly rough enough to bring this unruly crew to heel. Karswell must do it or it would never be done. The others he could manage, but the Manila men were dangerous. It was a strange type, with flat Tartar noses, small eyes, low, brutish foreheads, and lank, black hair like the American Indians. Their faces were of a dark coffee tint, and they were all men of powerful physique. Six of these fellows were on board, Leon, Blanco, Duranno, Santos, Lopez, and Marsolino, of whom Leon spoke English well and acted as interpreter for the rest. These were all placed in the mate's watch together with Watto, a handsome young Levantine, and Carlos, a Spaniard. The more tractable seamen were allotted to Taffir for the other watch. And so, on a beautiful July day, holiday makers upon the Kentish downs saw the beautiful craft as she swept past the Goodwins — never to be seen again, save once, by human eyes.

The Manila men appeared to submit to discipline, but there were lowering brows and sidelong glances which warned their officers not to trust them too far. Grumbles came from the forecastle as to the food and water — and the grumbling was perhaps not altogether unreasonable. But the mate was a man of hard nature and prompt resolution, and the malcontents got little satisfaction or sympathy from him. One of them, Carlos, the Spaniard, endeavoured to keep his bunk upon a plea of illness, but was dragged on deck by the mate, and triced up by the arms to the bulwarks. A few minutes afterward Capt. Smith's brother came on deck and informed the captain what was going on forward.

He came bustling up, and having examined the man he pronounced him to be really unwell and ordered him back to his bunk, prescribing some medicine for him. Such an incident would not tend to preserve discipline, or to uphold the mate's authority with the crew. On a later occasion this same Spaniard began fighting with Blanco, the biggest and most brutal of the Manila men, one using a knife and the other a handspike. The two mates threw themselves between them, and in the scuffle the first mate felled the Spaniard with his fist.

In the meantime the barque passed safely through the Bay and ran south as far as the latitude of Cape Blanco upon the African coast. The winds were light, and upon the 10th of September, when they had been six weeks out, they had only attained latitude 19 degrees south and longitude 36 degrees west. On that morning it was that the smouldering discontent burst into a most terrible flame.

The mate's watch was from one to four, during which dark hours he was left alone with the savage seamen whom he had controlled. No lion-tamer in a cage could be in more imminent peril, for death might be crouching in wait for him in any of those black shadows which mottled the moonlit deck. Night after night he had risked it until immunity had perhaps made him careless, but now at last it came. At six bells, or three in the morning—about the time when the first gray tinge of dawn was appearing in the Eastern sky, two of the mulattos, Blanco and Duranno, crept silently up behind the seaman, and struck him down with handspikes. Early, the English lad, who knew nothing of the plot, was looking out on the forecastle head at the time. Above the humming of the foresail above him, and the lapping of the water, he heard a sudden crash, and the voice of the mate calling murder. He ran aft, and found Duranno, with horrible persistence, still beating the mate about the head. When he attempted to interfere, the fellow ordered him sternly into the deckhouse, and he obeyed. In the deckhouse, the Norwegian carpenter and Candereau, the French seaman, were sleeping, both of whom were among the honest men. The boy Early told them what had occurred, his story being corroborated by the screeches of the mate from the outside. The carpenter ran out and found the unfortunate fellow with his arm broken and his face horribly mutilated.

"Who's that?" he cried, as he heard steps approaching.

"It's me — the carpenter."

"For God's sake get me into the cabin!"

The carpenter had stooped with the intention of doing so, but Marsolino, one of the conspirators, hit him on the back of the neck and knocked him down. The blow was not a dangerous one, but the carpenter took it as a sign that he should mind his own business, for he went back with impotent tears to his deckhouse. In the meanwhile, Blanco, who was the giant of the party, with the help of another mutineer, had raised Karswell, and hurled him, still yelling for help, over the bulwarks into the sea. He had been the first attacked, but he was not the first to die.

The first of those below to hear the dreadful summons from the deck was the captain's brother, George Smith — the one who had come for a pleasure trip. He ran up the companion and had his head beaten to pieces with handspikes as he emerged. Of the personal characteristics of this pleasure tripper, the only item which has been handed down is the grim fact that he was so slight that one man was able to throw his dead body overboard. The captain had been aroused at the same time and had rushed from his room into the cabin. Thither he was followed by Leon, Watto, and Lopez, who stabbed him to death with their knives. There remained only Taffir, the second mate, and his adventures may be treated with less reticence, since they were happier in their outcome.

He was awakened in the first gray of dawn by the sounds of smashing and hammering upon the companion. To so experienced a seaman those sounds at such an hour could have carried but one meaning, and that the most terrible which an officer at sea can ever learn. With a sinking heart he sprang from his bunk and rushed to the companion. It was choked by the sprawling figure of the captain's brother, upon whose head a rain of blows was still descending. In trying to push his way up, Taffir received a crack which knocked him backwards. Half distracted, he rushed back into the cabin and turned down the lamp, which was smoking badly — a graphic little touch which helps us to realize the agitation of the last hand which lit it. He then caught sight of the body of the captain, pierced with many stabs and lying in his blood-mottled nightgown upon the carpet. Horrified at the sight, he ran back into his berth and locked the door, waiting in a helpless quiver of apprehension for the next move of the mutineers. He may not have been of a very virile character, but the circumstances were enough to shake the most stout-hearted. It is not an hour at which a man is at his best, that chill hour of the opening dawn, and to have seen the two men, with whom he had supped the night before, lying in their blood, seems to have completely unnerved him. Shivering and weeping, he listened with straining ears for the footsteps which would be the forerunners of death.

At last they came, and of half a dozen men at least, clumping heavily down the brass-clamped steps of the companion. A hand beat roughly upon his door and ordered him out. He knew that his frail lock was no protection, so he turned the key and stepped forth. It might well have frightened a stouter man, for the murderers were all there, Leon, Carlos, Santos, Blanco, Duranno, Watto, dreadful-looking folk, most of them, at the best of times, but now, armed with their dripping knives and crimson cudgels, and seen in that dim morning light, as terrible a group as ever a writer of romance conjured up in his imagination. The Manila men stood in a silent semi-circle round the door, with their savage Mongolian faces turned upon him.

"What are you going to do with me?" he cried. "Are you going to kill me?" He tried to cling to Leon as he spoke, for as the only one who could speak English he had become the leader.

"No," said Leon, "we are not going to kill you. But we have killed the captain and the mate. Nobody on board knows anything of navigation. You must navigate us to where we can land."

The trembling mate, hardly believing the comforting assurance of safety, eagerly accepted the commission.

"Where shall I navigate you to?" he asked.

There was a whispering in Spanish among the dark-faced men, and it was Carlos who answered in broken English.

"Take up River Platte," said he. "Good country! Plenty Spanish!" And so it was agreed.

And now a cold fit of disgust seemed to have passed

through those callous ruffians, for they brought down
mops and cleaned out the cabin. A rope was slung
round the captain and he was hauled on deck, Taffir, to
his credit be it told, interfering to impart some decency
to the ceremony of his burial. "There goes the captain!"
cried Watto, the handsome Levantine lad, as he heard
the splash of the body. "He'll never call us names any
more!" Then all hands were called into the saloon, with
the exception of Candereau, the Frenchman, who
remained at the wheel. Those who were innocent had
to pretend approval of the crime to save their own lives.
The captain's effects were laid out upon the table and
divided into seventeen shares. Watto insisted that it
should only be eight shares, as only eight were concerned in the mutiny, but Leon with greater sagacity
argued that everyone should be equally involved in the
crime by taking their share of the booty. There were
money and clothes to divide, and a big box of boots
which represented some little commercial venture of
the captain's. Everyone was stamping about in a new
pair. The actual money came to about ten pounds
each, and the watch was set aside to be sold and divided
later. Then the mutineers took permanent possession of
the cabin, the course of the ship was altered for South
America, and the ill-fated barque began the second
chapter of her infamous voyage.

The cargo had been broached and the decks were
littered with open cases of champagne, from which
everyone helped himself as he passed. There was a
fusillade of popping corks all day, and the air was full of
the faint, sweet, sickly smell of the wine. The second
mate was nominally commander, but he was a commander without the power to command. From morning
to night he was threatened and insulted, and it was

only Leon's interference, and the well-grounded con-
viction that they could never make the land without
him, which saved him from their daily menaces. They
gave a zest to their champagne carousals by brandish-
ing their knives in his face.

All the honest men were subjected to the same
treatment. Santos and Watto came to the Norwegian
carpenter's whetstone to sharpen their knives, explaining to him as they did so that they would soon use them
on his throat. Watto, the handsome lad, declared that
he had already killed sixteen men. He wantonly stabbed
the inoffensive Chinese steward through the fleshy part
of the arm. Santos said to Candereau, the Frenchman:
"In two or three days I shall kill you!"

"Kill me then!" cried Candereau with spirit.

"This knife," said the bully, "will serve you the
same that it has the captain."

There seems to have been no attempt upon the part
of the nine honest men to combine against the eight
rogues. As they were all of different races and spoke
different languages, it is not surprising that they were
unable to make head against the armed and unanimous
mutineers.

And then there befell one of those incidents which
break the monotony of long sea voyages. The topsails
of a ship showed above the horizon and soon then rose
her hull. Her course would take her across their bows,
and the mate asked leave to hail her, as he was doubtful
as to his latitude.

"You may do so," said Leon. "But if you say a word
about us you are a dead man."

The strange ship hauled her yard aback when she
saw that the other wished to speak her, and the two lay

rolling in the Atlantic swell within a hundred yards of each other.

"We are the *Friend,* of Liverpool," cried an officer. "Who are you?"

"We are the *Louisa,* seven days out from Dieppe for Valparaiso," answered the unhappy mate, repeating what the mutineers whispered to him. The longitude was asked and given, and the two vessels parted company. With yearning eyes the harassed man looked at the orderly decks and the well-served officer of the Liverpool ship, while he in turn noticed with surprise those signs of careless handling which would strike the eye of a sailor in the rig and management of the *Flowery Land.* Soon the vessel was hull down upon the horizon, and in an hour the guilty ship was again alone in the vast ring of the ocean.

This meeting was very nearly being a fatal one to the mate, for it took all Leon's influence to convince the other ignorant and suspicious seamen that they had not been betrayed. But a more dangerous time still was before him. It must have been evident to him that when they had made their landfall, then was the time when he was no longer necessary to the crew, and when they were likely to silence him forever. That which was their goal was likely to prove his death warrant. Every day brought him nearer to this inevitable crisis, and then at last on the night of the 2nd of October the lookout man reported land ahead. The ship was at once put about, and in the morning the South American coast was a dim haze upon the western horizon. When the mate came up on deck he found the mutineers in earnest conclave about the fore-hatch, and their looks and gestures told him that it was his fate which was being debated.

Leon was again on the side of mercy. "If you like to kill the carpenter and the mate, you can: I shall not do it," said he. There was a sharp difference of opinion upon the matter, and the poor, helpless mate waited like a sheep near a knot of butchers.

"What are they going to do with me?" he cried to Leon, but received no reply. "Are they going to kill me?" he asked Marsolino.

"I am not, but Blanco is," was the discouraging reply.

However, the thoughts of the mutineers were happily diverted by other things. First they clewed up the sails and dropped the boats alongside. The mate having been deposed from his command, there was no commander at all, so that everything was chaos. Some got into the boats and some remained upon the decks of the vessel. The mate found himself in one boat which contained Watto, Paul the Sclavonian, Early the ship's boy, and the Chinese cook. They rowed a hundred yards away from the ship, but were recalled by Blanco and Leon. It shows how absolutely the honest men had lost their spirit, that though they were four to one in this particular boat they merely returned when they were recalled. The Chinese cook was ordered on deck, and the others were allowed to float astern. The unfortunate steward had descended into another boat, but Duranno pushed him overboard. He swam for a long time, begging hard for his life, but Leon and Duranno pelted him with empty champagne bottles from the deck until one of them struck him on the head and sent him to the bottom. The same men took Cassap, the little Chinese boy, into the cabin. Candereau, the French sailor, heard him cry out: "Finish me quickly then!" and they were the last words that he ever spoke.

In the meantime the carpenter had been led into the hold by the other mutineers and ordered to scuttle the ship. He bored four holes forward and four aft, and the water began to pour in. The crew sprang into the boats, one small one and one large one, the former in tow of the latter. So ignorant and thoughtless were they that they were lying alongside as the ship settled down in the water, and would infallibly have been swamped if the mate had not implored them to push off. The Chinese cook had been left on board, and had clambered into the tops so that his gesticulating figure was almost the last that was seen of the ill-omened *Flowery Land* as she settled down under the leaping waves. Then the boats, well laden with plunder, made slowly for the shore.

It was four in the afternoon upon the 4th of October that they ran their boats upon the South American beach. It was a desolate spot, so they tramped inland, rolling along with the gait of seamen ashore, their bundles upon their shoulders. Their story was that they were the shipwrecked crew of an American ship from Peru to Bordeaux. She had foundered a hundred miles out, and the captain and officers were in another boat which had parted company. They had been five days and nights upon the sea.

Toward evening they came upon the *estancia* of a lonely farmer to whom they told their tale, and from whom they received every hospitality. Next day they were all driven over to the nearest town of Roche. Candereau and the mate got an opportunity of escaping that night, and within twenty-four hours their story had been told to the authorities, and the mutineers were all in the hands of the police.

Of the twenty men who had started from London,

in the *Flowery Land,* six had met their deaths from
violence. There remained fourteen, of whom eight
were mutineers, and six were destined to be the witnesses against them. No more striking example could
be given of the long arm and steel hand of the British
law than that within a very few months this mixed
crew, Sclavonian, Negro, Manila men, Norwegian,
Turk, and Frenchman, gathered on the shore of the
distant Argentine, were all brought face to face at the
Central Criminal Court in the heart of London town.

The trial excited great attention on account of the
singular crew and the monstrous nature of their crimes.
The death of the officers did less to rouse the prejudice
of the public and to influence the jury than the callous
murder of the unoffending Chinaman. The great
difficulty was that of apportioning the blame amongst
so many men and of determining which had really been
active in the shedding of blood. Taffir, the mate; Early,
the ship's boy; Candereau, the Frenchman, and
Anderson, the carpenter, all gave their evidence, some
incriminating one and some another. After a very
careful trial, five of them, Leon, Blanco, Watto,
Duranno, and Lopez, were condemned to death. They
were all Manila men, with the exception of Watto, who
came from the Levant. The oldest of the prisoners was
only five and twenty years of age. They took their
sentence in a perfectly callous fashion, and immediately
before it was pronounced Leon and Watto laughed
heartily because Duranno had forgotten the statement
which he had intended to make. One of the prisoners
who had been condemned to imprisonment was at once
heard to express a hope that he might be allowed to
have Blanco's boots.

The sentence of the law was carried out in front of

Newgate upon the 22nd of February. Five ropes jerked
convulsively for an instant, and the tragedy of the
Flowery Land had reached its fitting consummation.

The Duello in France

THERE is a clause in one of the innumerable codes of law drawn up in France for the purpose of checking, or at least regulating, the practice of duelling, which proclaims it to be illegal to fight a duel on any question which may not be assessed at the money value of twopence-halfpenny. This limitation, modest as it appears, seems to have been too drastic for the tastes of the people to whom it was addressed, and the long roll of the single combats of the past contain many which could not possibly trace their origin to any question so weighty. The blend of the many high-spirited nations which go to make up the French people, of the Gaul, the Armorican, the Frank, the Burgundian, the Norman, the Goth, has produced a race who appear to have the combative spirit more highly developed that any other European nation. In spite of the incessant wars which make up the history of France, the record of private combat and bloodshed is an unbroken one, stretching back in a long red stream through the ages, sometimes narrow, sometimes broad, occasionally reaching such a flood as can only be ascribed to a passing fit of universal homicidal mania. Recent events have shown that this national tendency is still as strong as ever, and that there is every prospect that the duello, when driven from every other European country, may still find a home among a gallant people whose solicitude for their honour makes them occasionally a trifle neglectful of their intelligence.

The duello is undoubtedly in its origin a religious ceremony, and is the direct descendant of those judicial combats, where Providence was on the side of the sharpest lance and truest sword. To the fierce nations who overran the Roman Empire, such a doctrine was a congenial one, and, if they neglected all other precepts of the Christianity of the day, to this dogma of the sanctity of force they gave their warmest support. Germans, Franks, Goths, Vandals, and particularly Burgundians, turned the Deity into a supreme camp-marshal, presiding over their contests and adjudicating upon their disputes. From those distant centuries, the clash of sword-blades rises louder than the murmur of prayer. Dimly we catch glimpses of struggling men, clad in chain armour and leather, who champion causes, now of less weight than the falling leaves, but then all-important in the minds of men. A gallant young Ingelgerius, early Count of Anjou, cuts off the head of a slanderous Gontran, and the honour of the Countess of Gaston is saved. Or the Queen Gundeberge is freed from all stain by the courteous and hard-hitting cousin, who smites the lying Adalulf to the earth. In these fierce ages, the duel played a part often abused and yet not wholly useless. In the midst of chaos, it started up as a law, a rule, if it were but an unreasoning and fickle one. It is clear at least that no injured lady need lack a champion—more probable, indeed, that many champions were lacking an injured lady.

Gradually, as chivalry sprang up and imposed its ordinances and modes of thought upon the upper classes, the single combat in search of honour came to supplement the judicial duel. For centuries, they continue side by side. Young English knights, with patches over their eyes, spur out from the ranks of armies and exchange thrusts with French cavaliers as hotheaded as themselves. The Scotchman Seaton rides up to the gates of Paris, and having, in accordance with his vow, hurtled and smashed for half an hour with all the French knights whom he can see, he withdraws at last with a courteous "Thanks, gentlemen; many thanks." Thirty English must needs fight thirty Bretons at Ploermel and get well beaten for their pains. Seven other Englishmen have no better luck at Montendre. Everywhere in the public quarrel, as well as in private feud, there is the same tale of challenge and of acceptance.

The chronicles of the combats of chivalry do not, however, entirely obscure those of the law. The well-known and dramatic contest between Montargis and the hound occurred when the fourteenth century was already drawing to a close. As late, however, as the year 1547 occurred the famous trial by contest between Chasteneraye and Jarnac which is at once one of the last and one of the best known of the series.

Chasteneraye and Jarnac, both peers of France, had fallen out over the virtue of the latter's mother-in-law. The king had interested himself in the matter, and it was finally settled that the whole question should be referred to the arbitrament of arms. As it chanced, Chasteneraye was one of the first swordsmen in France, so that Jarnac exhausted his ingenuity in devising some abstruse and little-known weapon by means of which he might be more on an equality with his adversary. The names of thirty such arms were drawn up and submitted to the judges, who, however, to Jarnac's despair, laid them all aside and decided upon the sword. In his difficulty, he sought the advice of a tried old Italian swordsman, who bade him be of good heart and confided to him a secret trick of swordsmanship devised by himself and never before taught to mortal man. Armed with this horrid ruse, Jarnac repaired to the scene of the encounter, where, in the presence of the king, Henry II, and all the high officials of the kingdom, the two litigants were put face to face. Chasteneraye, confident in his skill, pressed hotly upon the less experienced Jarnac, when suddenly the latter, to the astonishment of the spectators, put in such a cut as had never before been seen and severed the tendon of his enemy's left leg. An instant later, by a repetition of the same stroke, he cut the sinew of the right one, and the unfortunate Chasteneraye fell hamstrung to the earth. In this sore plight, he still continued upon his knees to make passes at his antagonist and to endeavour to carry on the combat. His sword, however, was quickly struck from his grasp, and he lay at the mercy of his conqueror. The wily Jarnac was disposed, very much against the customs of the time, to grant him his life; but the humiliation was too much for the beaten and crippled man, and, refusing all assistance, he allowed himself to bleed to death. The "coup de Jarnac" in sword-play still remains as a memorial of this encounter.

The actual duello, as we understand it, appears to have been an importation from Italy. During the fifty years which terminated with Francis I, the French troops had been quartered without intermission in Italy and had brought back to their native country many of the least admirable traits of the Italians. An epidemic

of bloodshed and murder broke out in France at the
beginning of the sixteenth century. The life of Duprat,
Baron of Vitaux, may be taken as typical of that of
many another young high-born ruffian of the period.
This interesting person has been named by Brantome
"the paragon of France," so that the study of his life
gives us an interesting opportunity of knowing the sort
of man who won the applause of the populace at the
latter end of the middle ages. While yet in his teens, he
slew the young Baron de Soupez, who had certainly
given him some provocation by smiting him on the
head with a candlestick. His next exploit was the death
of a certain Gounelieu, with whom there had been a
family quarrel. This deed led to his banishment, but he
was speedily back again, and with two accomplices set
upon the Baron de Mittaud and cut him to pieces in the
streets of Paris. The king's favourite, Guart, ventured
to oppose the calm request that Duprat should receive a
free pardon for all these enormities. For this offence, he
was attacked in his own house and murdered by the
young desperado. This crime proved, however, to be
the last of his short but eventful life, for he was shortly
afterwards slain himself by the brother of one of his
former victims. "He was a very fine man," says
Brantome, "though there were some who said that he
did not kill his people properly" — *"Il ne tuait pas bien
ses gens."* The career of this ruffian marks the transition
period when the regulated combats of chivalry had died
out but the stringent laws of the duello had not yet been
formed.

Towards the end of the sixteenth century, however,
during the reign of Henry III, the duello began to
conform to established rules. The foolish custom of
seconds engaging in the quarrels of their principals had

been introduced from Italy, and the single challenge led occasionally to a small battle. The encounter between Caylus and D'Entragues, two well-known courtiers, has been narrated at some length by the chroniclers. Riberac and Schomberg were seconds to D'Estragues, Maugerin and Livaret to Caylus.

"Hadn't we better reconcile these gentlemen instead of allowing them to kill one another?" says Riberac to Maugerin.

"Sir," replies the other, "I did not come here to string beads, but to fight."

"And with whom?" asks Riberac.

"With you, to be sure."

Instantly, they flew at each other and ran each other through. Schomberg and Livaret in the meantime had come to blows, with the result that the former fell dead, while the latter was wounded in the face. Caylus meanwhile had been mortally wounded, and his opponent had received a sword-thrust. This single encounter ended, therefore, in the immediate death of four men, while the other two were badly crippled. Whatever charge might be levelled against the French duel of those days, it could not be said that the participants were not in earnest.

In the reign of Henry IV, duelling reached its highest point. It has been estimated that during his reign no fewer than 4,000 nobles fell victims to the fashion. Chavalier narrates that in Limousin alone, in the space of seven months, 120 were actually killed. The smallest difference of opinion led to an appeal to arms. At no time would the remark of Montesquieu be more true, that if three Frenchmen had been set down in the Libyan Desert, two would instantly have paired off, and the third resolved himself into a second.

Strange use was made occasionally of the right of the challenged to fix upon the weapon which should be used, and the conditions under which the contest should be decided. Thus we hear of a very small man who insisted upon his gigantic adversary wearing a stock or collar all girt round with spikes, so that, being unable to bend his neck, he was unable to keep his eye upon his little opponent. Another duellist insisted upon the use of a cuirass which had a little hole over the heart, he being well practised in that particular thrust. Unfair as such conditions might seem, they at least gave the advantage to the challenged, and so made it a more serious matter to fix a quarrel upon a man.

Now and then a man arose so brave that he dared to refuse to fight. Monsieur de Reuly, a young officer in the army, quoted the law of God and of man as a reason for his refusal. His adversary, however, under the impression that he had a poltroon to deal with, lay in wait for him in the street with a friend and set upon him. The young officer, however, ran them both through the body, and so vindicated his right to remain at peace.

Lord Herbert of Cherbury, our ambassador at the court of Louis XIII, was himself a noted duellist, and has recorded some interesting examples of the favour in which the practice was held in French society. "All things being ready for the ball," says he, "and everyone being in their place and I myself next to the queen, expecting when the dancers would come in, one knocked at the door somewhat louder than became, I thought, a very civil person: when he came in there was, I remember, a sudden whisper among the ladies, saying, 'C'est Monsieur Balaguy.' Whereupon I also saw the ladies and gentlemen, one after the other, invite him to sit near them: and what is more, when one lady had his company a while, another would say, 'You have enjoyed him long enough, I must have him now.' At which bold civility of them, though I was astonished, yet it added to my wonder that his person could not be thought at most but ordinary handsome: his hair, which was cut very short, half grey: his doublet but of sackcloth cut to his skin, and his breeches but of plain grey cloth. Informing myself by some by-standers who he was, I was told that he was one of the gallantest men in the world, as having killed eight or nine men in single fight, and that for that reason the ladies made so much of him: it being the manner of all French women to cherish gallant men, as thinking they could not make so much of any one else with safety of their honour." A little later, we find Lord Herbert himself endeavouring to fix a quarrel on this same Balaguy, but without the success which his efforts deserved. His picture, however, of the sombre duellist moving about among the gay dresses of the ball-room is a vivid one.

Of this epoch, too, was De Boutteville, famous for his innumerable duels and interminable moustaches. "Do you still think of life?" said the Bishop of Nantes as he ascended the scaffold which he had so often deserved. "I think only of my moustaches — the finest in France," answered the doomed desperado.

Louis XIV endeavoured, and with some success, to limit the pernicious habit. His far-reaching ambitions could only be attained through the blood of his subjects, and he grudged every life which was sacrificed in any but the public quarrel. Indeed, through his long reign there was so much work for the rapiers of his *noblesse* over the frontiers that the most pugnacious of them must have found his thirst for strife more than gratified.

Yet in spite of edict and penalty, we find the practice still full of vitality. Even the pacific La Fontaine fights a captain of dragoons because he visits his wife too often, and then, in a moment of repentance, wishes to fight him again because he refuses to visit her. In this reign, too, the gallant one-legged Marquis de Rivard, when challenged by a person of the name of Madaillon, sent his adversary a case of surgical instruments, with an intimation that he was ready to meet him as soon as he had placed himself on an equal footing with him.

During the dissolute reign of Louis XV, duelling flourished as merrily as ever. Within the very precincts of the palace, and at midday on the quay of the Tuileries, there were fatal encounters. Financiers encroached on the time-honoured privileges of the *noblesse,* and the Scotchman Law, of Mississippi fame, was as skilful with his weapons as with his figures. The Duke de Richelieu, Du Vighan, St. Evremont, and St. Foix are among the most notorious fighting men of the day. The truculence of the last was modified by a vein of humour. On one occasion, he received a challenge for having asked a gentleman why it was that he smelled so confoundedly. St. Foix, contrary to his usual habit, refused the invitation. "Were you to slay me, it would not make you smell any sweeter," said he, "whereas if I were to slay you, you would smell worse than ever."

The short and disastrous reign of Louis XVI pro-duced at least two remarkable duellists, the petticoated Chevalier d'Eon, and the mulatto St. George. D'Eon died in London as late as 1810, and though there was no doubt as to his true sex, no satisfactory reason was ever given for the whim which made him for nearly a quarter of a century attire himself in women's clothes.

The black St. George was at once the best fencer and the best pistol shot of his day, and won his reputation in many meetings. In spite of his fame as a duellist, he is said to have been a very inoffensive man and to have avoided quarrels as far as he might. One of the most wholesale challenges on record dates from this period, when the Marquis de Tenteniac, being rebuked for sitting too far forward at the wings, considered himself to be slighted by the audience. "Ladies and gentlemen," said he, "with your permission, a piece will be performed to-morrow called 'The insolence of the pit chastised,' in as many acts as may be desired, by the Marquis de Tenteniac." The peaceable pit took no notice of the bellicose nobleman's challenge.

The terrible wars of Napoleon put an end to duelling for the time, but the Restoration brought it forward again with renewed vigour. What with social quarrels, the political rancour between the Buonapartists and the Legitimists, and the international feud between Frenchmen and the troops occupying France, there was seldom so fine a field for the man who wished to pick a quarrel. On the one hand, the old officers of Napoleon were driven to frenzy by the sight of the officers of the allied armies in their capital and endeavoured to avenge their defeat in the battlefield by their prowess in the Bois de Boulogne. On the other, the young Bourbonist courtiers were ready to answer with rapier stab and pistol bullet to the reproach that for the sake of a dynasty they had sacrificed their country.

Count Gronow in his interesting reminiscences gives a lively picture of the Paris of the day. International duels were things of daily occurrence, and generally terminated in favour of the Frenchman as being more skilled in the use of weapons. Their hatred was most bitter against the Prussians, and without the formalities of the duel it was no uncommon thing for a group of French officers to go down to the Café Foy, in the Palais Royal, which was the usual Prussian rendezvous, for the purpose of having a general struggle with its inmates. In one of these contests as many as fourteen Prussians and ten Frenchmen were slain outright. The English lost many promising young officers at this time in Paris. Gronow, however, who was present at the time, gives many instances where the result was in the favour of our countrymen. In the south, at Bordeaux, where the Frenchmen came across the Garonne for the express purpose of insulting our officers, they lost so many men that they at last gave up the practice. Dr. Millingen, whose work upon duelling is a storehouse of information upon the subject, was himself at Bordeaux at the time and has given some details as to these encounters. The French, according to this authority, were incomparably the better swordsmen, but the young Englishmen, relying upon their superior bodily strength, would throw themselves upon their antagonists with such a supreme disregard for the science of the thing that they not unfrequently succeeded in cutting down their bewildered opponents.

That the duello has immense vitality in France is evidenced by the fact that it succeeded in surviving its adoption by the lower orders during the twenty years which followed Waterloo. What the edicts of kings could not abolish ran a great risk of dying of ridicule when rival grocers took to calling each other out, and a bath-keeper sent a cartel to a crockeryware man for having sold him a damaged stove. Nor were these plebeian encounters less earnest occasionally than those of warriors and statesmen. At Douai, a brazier and a woollendraper were both left dead upon the ground after an encounter with sabres. All disputes of every sort were reduced to the same foolish arbitrament. We hear of critics firing four shots at each other in order to decide the relative merits of the classical and the romantic schools of fiction. Dumas fights Gaillardet the playwright, and in endeavouring to decide the authorship of one drama runs a risk of being an actor in another. Finally, at Bordeaux, we have a case of a captain of dragoons going out with an old-clothesman, and narrowly escaping lynching at the hands of the infuriated Israelites.

The well-known duel between M. Dulong and General Bugeaud may be taken as a final example of the brutality and folly inseparable from the custom. Dulong was a peaceable lawyer and a member of the House of Deputies. Bugeaud was a soldier and a famous pistol-shot. Dulong in his capacity as member of the legislative body ventures to make some adverse criticism in the house and is instantly challenged by the fire-eater. In vain he protests that no personal allusion was intended. He must go out or be under a social ban. Out they go accordingly, and the trained pistol-shot kills his civilian opponent before the latter discharges his weapon. Such a result still leaves us facing the difficulty which occurred to the Oxford mathematician on reading *Paradise Lost*. What is proved by that successful shot, and how it affects the original dispute, must ever remain a mystery.

An Englishman can scarcely be censorious when he speaks of the duels of the past, for his own chronicles are too often stained by encounters as desperate as any across the Channel. The time at last has come, however, when the duel is as much an anachronism in our own country, and in the settled states of the Union, as judicial torture or the burning of witches. Only when France has attained the same position can she claim to be on a par with the Anglo-Saxon nations in the quality of her civilization.

A New Light on
Old Crimes

SYCHIC SCIENCE, though still in its infancy, has already reached a point where we can dissect many of those occurrences which were regarded as inexplicable in past ages, and can classify and even explain them — so far as any ultimate explanation of anything is possible. It would be interesting, therefore, to survey some of those cases which stand on record in our law courts, and have been variously explained in the past as being either extraordinary coincidences or as interpositions of Providence. The latter phrase may well represent a fact, but people must learn that no such thing has ever been known as an interposition of Providence save through natural law, and that when it has seemed inexplicable and miraculous it is only because the law has not yet been understood. All miracles come under exact law, but the law, like all natural laws, is itself divine and miraculous.

We will endeavour in recounting these cases, which can only be done in the briefest fashion, to work from the simpler to the more complex — from that which may have depended upon the natural but undefined powers of the subconscious self, through all the range of clairvoyance and telepathy, until we come to that which seems beyond all question to be influenced by the spirit of the dead. There is one case, that of Owen Parfitt, of Shepton Mallet, in Somersetshire, which may form a starting-point, since it is really impossible to say whether it was psychic or not; but if it were not, it forms one of the most piquant mysteries which ever came before the British public.

This old fellow was a seaman, a kind of John Silver, who lived in the piratical days of the eighteenth century and finally settled down, upon what were usually considered to have been ill-gotten gains, about the year 1760, occupying a comfortable cottage on the edge of the little Somerset town. His sister kept house for him, but she was herself too infirm to look after the rheumatic old mariner, so a neighbour named Susanna Snook used to come in by the day and help to care for him. It was observed that Parfitt went periodically to Bristol, and that he returned with money, but how he gained it was his secret. He appears to have been a secretive and wicked old creature, with many strange tales of wild doings, some of which related to the West Coast of Africa, and possibly to the slave trade. Eventually his infirmity increased upon him. He could no longer get farther than his garden, and seldom left the great chair in which he was placed every day by the ministering Susanna Snook, just outside the porch of the cottage.

Then one summer morning, June 6, 1768, an extraordinary thing happened. He had been deposited as usual, with a shawl round his shoulders, while the hard-working Susanna darted back to her own cottage near-by. She was away for half an hour. When she returned she found, to her amazement, that the old seaman had disappeared. His sister was wringing her hands in great bewilderment over the shawl, which still remained upon the chair, but as to what became of the old reprobate nothing has ever been learned from that day to this. It should be emphasized that he was practically unable to walk and was far too heavy to be easily carried.

The alarm was at once given, and as the haymaking was in full swing the countryside was full of workers, who were ready to declare that even if he could have walked he could not have escaped their observation upon the roads. A search was started, but it was interrupted by a sudden and severe storm, with thunder and heavy rain. In spite of the weather, there was a general alarm for twenty-four hours, which failed to discover the least trace of the missing man. His unsavoury character, some reminiscences of the Obi men and Voodoo cult of Africa, and the sudden thunderstorm, all combined to assure the people of Somerset that the devil had laid his claws upon the old seaman; nor has any natural explanation since those days set the matter in a more normal light. There were hopes once that this had been attained when, in the year 1813, some human bones were discovered in the garden of a certain Widow Lockyer, who lived within two hundred yards of the old man's cottage. Susanna Snook was still alive, and gave evidence at the inquiry, but just as it began to appear that perhaps the old man had been coaxed away and murdered, a surgeon from Bristol shut down the whole matter by a positive declaration that the bones were those of a woman. So the affair rests till to-day.

No psychic explanation can be accepted in any case until all reasonable normal solutions have been exhausted. It is possible that those visits to Bristol were connected with blackmail, and that some deeper villain in the background found means to silence that dangerous tongue. But how was it done? It is a freakish, insoluble borderland case, and there we must leave it.

Passing on to a more definite example, let us take the case of the murder of Maria Marten, which was for a long time a favourite subject when treated at village fairs under the name of "The Mystery of the Red Barn." Maria Marten was murdered in the year 1827 by a young farmer named Corder, who should have married her but failed to do so, preferring to murder her in order to conceal the result of their illicit union. His ingenious method was to announce that he was about to marry the girl, and then at the last hour shot her dead and buried her body. He then disappeared from the neighbourhood, and gave out that he and she were secretly wedded and were living together at some unknown address.

The murder was on May 18, 1827, and for some time the plan was completely successful, the crime being more effectually concealed because Corder had left behind him instructions that the barn should be filled up with stock. The rascal sent home a few letters purporting to be from the Isle of Wight, explaining that Maria and he were living together in great contentment. Some suspicion was aroused by the fact that the postmarks of these letters were all from London, but none the less the matter might have been overlooked had it not been for the unusual action of an obscure natural law which had certainly never been allowed for in Mr. Corder's calculations.

Mrs. Marten, the girl's mother, dreamed upon three nights running that her daughter had been murdered. This in itself might count for little, since it may have only reflected her vague fears and distrust. The dreams, however, were absolutely definite. She saw in them the red barn, and even the very spot in which the remains had been deposited. The latter detail is of great importance, since it disposes of the idea that the incident could have arisen from the girl having told her mother that she had an assignation there. The dreams occurred in March 1828, ten months after the crime, but it was the middle of April before the wife was able to persuade her husband to act upon such evidence. At last she broke down his very natural scruples, and permission was given to examine the barn, now cleared of its contents. The woman pointed to the spot and the man dug. A piece of shawl was immediately exposed, and eighteen inches below it the body itself was discovered, the horrified searcher staggering in a frenzy out of the ill-omened barn. The dress, the teeth, and some small details were enough to establish the identification.

The villain was arrested in London, where he had become, by marriage, the proprietor of a girls' school, and was engaged, at the moment of capture, in ticking off the minutes for the correct boiling of the breakfast eggs. He set up an ingenious defence, by which he tried to prove that the girl had committed suicide, but there was no doubt that it was a cold-blooded crime, for he had taken not only pistols, but also a pickaxe into the barn. This was the view which the jury took, and he was duly hanged, confessing his guilt in a half-hearted way before his execution. It is an interesting fact that the London schoolmistress, whom he had trapped into marriage by means of a specious advertisement in which he described himself as a "private gentleman, whose disposition is not to be exceeded," remained devotedly attached to him to the end.

Now here is a case about which there is no possible

doubt. The murder was unquestionably discovered by means of the triple dream, for which there could have been no natural explanation. There remain two psychic explanations. The one depends upon telepathy or thought-reading, a phenomenon which, of course, exists, as anyone can prove who experiments with it, but which has been stretched to most unreasonable lengths by those who would prefer any explanation to that which entails disembodied intelligence. It is, of course, within the bounds of remote possibility that the murderer thought of the girl's mother upon three successive nights and also upon the scene of the crime, thus connecting up the vision of one with the brain of the other. If any student thinks this the more probable explanation he is certainly entitled to accept it. On the other hand, there is a good deal of evidence that dreams, and especially early-in-the-morning dreams just before the final waking, do at times convey information which seems to come from other intelligences than our own. Taking all the facts, I am of opinion that the spirit of the dead woman did actually get in touch with the mind of the mother, and impressed upon her the true facts of her unhappy fate. It is to be remembered, however, that even those who advanced telepathy as an explanation of such a case are postulating a power which was utterly unknown to science until this generation, and which itself represents a great extension of our psychic knowledge. We must not allow it, however, to block our way to the further and more important advances which lie beyond it.

For purposes of comparison we will now take another dream case which is perfectly authentic. Upon February 8th, 1840, Edmund Norway, the chief officer of the ship *Orient,* at that time near St. Helena, dreamed a dream between the hours of 10 P.M. and 4 A.M. in which he saw his brother Nevell, a Cornish gentleman, murdered by two men. His brother was seen to be mounted. One of the assailants caught the horse's bridle and snapped a pistol twice, but no report was heard. He and his comrade then struck him several blows, and dragged him to the side of the road, where they left him. The road appeared to be a familiar one in Cornwall, but the house, which should have been on the right, came out upon the left in the visual picture. The dream was recorded in writing at the time, and was told to the other officers of the ship.

The murder had actually occurred, and the assassins, two brothers named Lightfoot, were executed on April 13th of that year, at Bodmin. In his confession the elder brother said: "I went to Bodmin on February 8th and met my brother . . . my brother knocked Mr. Norway down. He snapped a pistol at him twice, but it did not go off. He then knocked him down with the pistol. It was on the road to Wadebridge" (the road which had been seen in the dream). "We left the body in the water on the left side of the road coming to Wadebridge. My brother drew the body across the road to the watering." The evidence made it clear that the murder was committed between the hours of ten and eleven at night. As St. Helena is, roughly, in the same longitude as England, the time of the dream might exactly correspond with that of the crime.

These are the actual facts, and, though they may be explained, they cannot be explained away. It appears that Norway, the sailor, had been thinking of and writing to his landsman brother just before going to his bunk. This might possibly have made the subsequent vision more easy by bringing the two men into *rapport*.

There is a considerable body of evidence to prove that during sleep there is some part of us, call it the etheric body, the subconscious self, or what you will, which can detach itself and visit distant scenes, though the cut-off between sleeping and waking is so complete that it is very rarely that the memory of the night's experience is carried through. It can easily be conceived that the consciousness of the sailor, drawn to his brother by recent loving thoughts, went swiftly to him in his sleep, and was so shocked to witness his murder that it was able to carry the record through into his normal memory. The case would resolve itself, then, into one which depended upon the normal but unexplored powers of the human organism, and not upon any interposition from the spirit of the murdered man. Had the vision of the latter appeared alone, without the accompanying scene, it would have seemed more probable that it was indeed a post-mortem apparition.

For the next illustration we will turn to the records of American crime. In this case, a man named Mortensen owed a considerable sum of money, three thousand eight hundred dollars, to a company, which was represented by the secretary, Mr. Hay. The transaction occurred in Utah in the year 1901. Mortensen beguiled Hay to his private house late in the evening, and nothing more was heard of the unfortunate man. Mortensen's story was that he paid the money in gold, and that Hay had given him a receipt and had started home with the money, carried in glass jars. When the police visited Mortensen's house in the morning they were accompanied by Hay's father-in-law, an aged Mormon named Sharp, who said: "Where did you last see my son-in-law?"

"Here," answered Mortensen, indicating a spot outside his door.

"If that is the last place you saw him," said Sharp, "then that is where you killed him."

"How do you know he is dead?" asked Mortensen.

"I have had a vision," said Sharp, "and the proof is that within one mile of the spot where you are standing, his dead body will be dug up from the field."

There was snow on the ground at the time, and next morning, December 18th, a neighbour observed some blood-stains upon it not very far from Mortensen's house. They led to a mound shaped like a grave. The neighbour procured a spade, borrowing it from Mortensen himself, and speedily unearthed the body of Hay. There was a bullet wound at the back of his head. His valuables had been untouched, but the receipt which he was known to have carried to Mortensen's house afforded sufficient reason for the murder.

The whole crime seems to have been a very crude and elementary affair, and it is difficult to see how Mortensen could have hoped to save himself, unless, indeed, an immediate flight was in his mind. There could be no adequate defence, and the man was convicted and shot — the law of Utah giving the criminal the choice as to the fashion of his own death. The only interest in the affair is the psychic one, for again old Sharp repeated at the trial that in a vision he had learned the facts. It is not a very clear case, however, and may conceivably have been a bluff upon the part of the old man, who had formed his own opinion as to the character of his son-in-law, and his probable actions. Such a solution would, however, involve a very extraordinary coincidence.

The next case which I would cite is very much more convincing—in fact, it is final in its clear proof of psychic action, though the exact degree may be open to discussion. The facts seem to have been established beyond all possible doubt, though there is some slight confusion about the date. According to the account of Mr. Williams, of Cornwall, the chief actor, it was in the early days of May 1812 that he thrice in the same night had a remarkable dream. Mr. Williams was a man of affairs, and the superintendent of some great Cornish mines. He was familiar with the lobby of the House of Commons, into which his interests had occasionally led him. It was this lobby which he perceived clearly in his dream. His attention was arrested by a man in a snuff-coloured coat, with metal buttons, who loitered there. Presently there entered a small, brisk man in a blue coat and white waistcoat. As he passed, the first man whipped out a pistol and shot the other through the breast. In his dream Mr. Williams was made aware that the murdered man was Mr. Perceval, the Chancellor of the Exchequer. Mr. Williams was greatly impressed, and alarmed, by this dream, and he recounted it not only to his wife but also to several friends whom he met at the Godolphin mine next day, asking their advice whether he should go up to London and report the matter. To this they answered very naturally, but unfortunately as the event proved, that it was useless, and would only expose him to derision. On the thirteenth, about ten days after the dream, Mr. Williams narrates how his son, returning from Truro, rushed into the room, crying, "Oh, father, your dream has come true! Mr. Perceval has been shot in the House of Commons." The deed, as is well known, was committed by a man named Bellingham, who had some imaginary grievance. The dress of the two chief actors, and all the other details, proved to be exactly as foretold.

In an account in *The Times* sixteen years later it was stated that the vision was upon the actual night of the murder, which would reduce the case to ordinary clairvoyance, but the evidence is very strong that it was prophetic as well. Mr. Williams, writing in 1832, four years after *The Times* account, repeated the story once more as it is set forth here. His wife, his friends at the mine, his projected journey to London, and his recollection of his son's arrival with the news all corroborate his version of the affair.

Mr. Williams was of Welsh or Cornish stock, and predisposed to the psychic. In his busy life he could not develop it, yet at times his true innate powers could assert themselves. Why the vision should have been sent him is beyond our ken. Was it to prompt him to go to London, as he so nearly did, and try to turn the stream of fate? When one considers that in this instance the picture of the lobby of the House of Commons was presented to one of the very few men in Cornwall who would recognize the place when they saw it, it certainly suggests that the vision did not merely happen, but came for a definite purpose.

We shall now turn to some cases which were more clearly ultramundane in their nature. The first which I would choose is the murder of Sergeant Davies in the Highlands in the year 1749. Davies was part of the English garrison left in the north after the suppression of Prince Charlie's rising, and, like many of his comrades, he alleviated his exile by the excellent sport which the barren country afforded. Upon September 28th in that year he went shooting near Braemar without any attendant. The rancour of the recent war had to some extent died down, and in any case the sergeant, who was a powerful and determined man, feared no opponent. The result showed, however, that he was overbold, as he never returned from his expedition. Search parties were sent out, but months passed and there were still no signs of the missing soldier. Five years passed, and the mystery was still unsolved. At the end of that time, two Highlanders, Duncan Terig and Alex. Bain Macdonald, were arrested because the fowling-piece and some of the property of the lost man were found in their possession. The case rested mainly, however, upon some evidence which was as strange as any ever heard in a court of law.

A farm labourer named Alex. Macpherson, aged twenty-six, deposed that one night in the summer of 1750 — that is, some nine months after the sergeant's disappearance — he was lying awake in the barn where all the servants slept, when he saw enter a man dressed in blue, who came to his bedside and beckoned him to follow. Outside the door the figure turned and said: "I am Sergeant Davies." The apparition then pointed to a distant moss or swamp, and said: "You will find my bones there. Go and bury them at once, for I can have no peace, nor will I give you any, until my bones are buried, and you may get Donald Farquharson to help you." It then vanished.

Early next day Macpherson, according to his own account, went to the place indicated and, obeying the exact instructions received, he came straight upon the body, still wearing the blue regimental coat of Guise's Horse. Macpherson laid it upon the surface, dragging it out from the slime, but did not bury it. A few nights later the vision appeared to him once more as he lay in the barn, and reproached him with having failed to carry out the instructions given. Macpherson asked: "Who murdered you?" To this the apparition answered: "Duncan Terig and Alex. Macdonald," and vanished once more. Macpherson next day went to Farquharson and asked him to come and help bury the body, to which the latter agreed. It was accordingly done. No one else was told of the incident save only one friend, John Grewar, who was informed within two days of the burial.

This story was certainly open to criticism, as the arrest was in 1754, and the alleged apparition and subsequent burial in 1750, so that one would naturally ask why no information had been given during four years. On the other hand, one could imagine that these Celtic Highlanders were somewhat in the position of Irish peasants in an agrarian outrage. They were bound together against a common enemy, and would not act save under pressure. This pressure arrived when the two suspects were actually arrested, the murdered man's gear was found upon them, and direct inquiry was made from the folk in the neighbourhood. No ill-will was shown to exist between Macpherson and the accused men, nor was any motive alleged for so extraordinary a concoction. On the psychic side there are also some objections. One would have conceived that the sergeant might return, as others seem to have done, in order to identify his murderers, but in this case that was a secondary result, and the main one appears to have been the burial of his own remains. Spirits are not much concerned about their own bodies. Still, earthly prejudices die hard, and if Davies, sprung from a decent stock, yearned for a decent burial, it would surely not be an unnatural thing.

There was some corroboration for Macpherson's weird story. There were female quarters in this barn, and a woman worker, named Isabel Machardie, deposed that on the second occasion of the apparition she saw "something naked come in at the door and go straight to Macpherson's bed, which frightened her so much that she drew the clothes over her head." She added that when it appeared it came in a bowing posture, but she could not tell what it was. The next morning she asked Macpherson what it was that had troubled them the night before, and he answered that she might be easy, for it would trouble them no more.

There is a discrepancy here between the blue-coated figure of the first version and the "something naked" of the second, but the fact remained that the woman claimed to have seen something alarming, and to have alluded to it next day. Macpherson, however, could speak nothing but Gaelic, his evidence being interpreted to the court. Lockhart, the defending barrister, naturally asked in what tongue the vision spoke, to which Macpherson answered: "In as good Gaelic as ever I heard in Lochaber." "Pretty good for the ghost of an English sergeant," said Lockhart, and this facile retort made the court laugh, and finally brought about the acquittal of the prisoners, in spite of the more material proofs which could not be explained away. Later, both Lockhart and the advocate engaged with him, admitted their belief in the guilt of their clients.

As a matter of fact, Davies had fought at Culloden in April 1746, and met his end in September 1749, so that he had been nearly three and a half years in the Highlands, mixing in sport with the gillies, and it is difficult to suppose that he could not muster a few simple sentences of their language.

But apart from that, although our information shows that knowledge has to be acquired by personal effort, and not by miracle, in the after life, still it is to be so acquired, and if Sergeant Davies saw that it was only in a Gael that he would find those rare psychic gifts which would enable him to appear and to communicate (for every spirit manifestation must have a material basis), then it is not inconceivable that he would master the means during the ten months or so which elapsed before his reappearance. Presuming that Macpherson's story is true, it by no means follows that he was the medium, since any one of the sleepers in the barn might have furnished that nameless atmosphere which provides the correct conditions. In all such cases it is to be remembered that this atmosphere is rare, and that a spirit comes back not as it would or when it would, but as it can. Law, inexorable law, still governs every fresh annexe which we add to our knowledge, and only by defining and recognizing its limitations will we gain some dim perception of the conditions of the further life and its relation to the present one.

We now pass to a case where the spirit interposition seems to have been as clearly proved as anything could be. It was, it is true, some time ago, but full records are still available. In the year 1632 a yeoman named John Walker lived at the village of Great Lumley, some miles north of Durham. A cousin named Anne Walker kept house for him, and intimacy ensued, with the prospect of the usual results. John Walker greatly feared the scandal, and took diabolical steps to prevent it. He sent the young woman over to the town of

Chester-le-Street to the care of one Dame Carr. To this matron Anne Walker confessed everything, adding that Walker had used the ominous phrase "that he would take care both of her and of her child." One night at Dame Carr's door there appeared the sinister visage of Mark Sharp, a Blackburn collier, with a specious message which induced the girl to go with him into the dusk. She was never seen again. Walker, upon being appealed to by Dame Carr, said that it was all right, and that it was better in her condition that she should be among strangers. The old lady had her suspicions, but nothing could be done, and the days passed on.

A fortnight later a miller, named James Graham, was grinding corn in his mill at night some miles away. It was after midnight when he descended to the floor of the mill after putting a fresh fill of corn in the hopper. His exact experience, as preserved in the Bodleian Library at Oxford, was as follows:

The mill door being shut, there stood a woman in the midst of the floor, with her hair hanging down all bloody, with five large wounds on her head. He being much amazed began to bless himself, and at last asked her who she was and what she wanted. She answered, "I am the spirit of Anne Walker, who lived with John Walker. . . . He promised to send me to where I should be well looked to . . . and then I should come again and keep his house. I was one night sent away with Mark Sharp, who, upon a certain moor" (naming the place) "slew me with a pick such as men dig coal with and gave me these five wounds, and after threw my body into a coalpit hard by, and hid the pick under a bank, and his shoes and stockings being bloody he endeavoured to wash them, but seeing the blood would not part he hid them there."

The spirit ended by ordering the miller to reveal the truth on pain of being haunted.

In this case, as in the last, the message was not delivered. The horrified miller was so impressed that he would by no means be alone, but he shirked the delicate task which had been confided to him. In spite of all his precautions, however, he found himself alone one evening, with the result that the vision instantly reappeared, "very fierce and cruel," to use his description, and insisted that he should do as commanded. More obdurate than the Celtic Macpherson, the miller awaited a third summons, which came in so terrific a form in his own garden that his resistance was completely broken down, and so, four days before Christmas, he went to the nearest magistrate and lodged his deposition. Search was at once made, and the vision was justified in all particulars, which, it must be admitted, has not always been the case where information has seemed to come from beyond. The girl's body, the five wounds in the head, the pick, the bloodstained shoes and stockings were all found, and as the body was in a deep coalpit there seemed no normal means by which the miller could possibly have known the nature of the wounds unless he had himself inflicted them, which is hardly consistent either with the known facts, with his appearance as informer, or with the girl's admissions to Dame Carr.

John Walker and Mark Sharp were both arrested and were tried for murder at the Durham Assizes before Judge Davenport. It was shown that the miller was unknown, save by sight, to either prisoner, so that it could not be suggested that he had any personal reason for swearing away their lives by a concocted tale. The trial was an extraordinary one, for there seems to have been a psychic atmosphere such as has never been recorded in a prosaic British court of law. The foreman of the jury, a Mr. Fairbairn, declared in an affidavit that he saw during the trial the "likeness of a child standing upon Walker's shoulder." This might be discounted as being the effect upon an emotional nature of the weird evidence to which he had listened, but it received a singular corroboration from the judge, who wrote afterwards to a fellow-lawyer, Mr. Serjeant Hutton, of Goldsborough, that he himself was aware of a figure such as Fairbairn described, and that during the whole proceedings he was aware of a most uncanny and unusual sensation for which he could by no means account. The verdict was guilty, and the two men were duly executed.

The array of responsible witnesses in this case was remarkable. There was the judge himself, Mr. Fairbairn, with his affidavit, Mr. James Smart, Mr. William Lumley, of Great Lumley, and others. Altogether, it is difficult to see how any case could be better authenticated, and I have no doubt myself that the facts were as stated, and that this single case is enough to convince an unprejudiced mind of the continuance of individuality and of the penetrability of that screen which separates us from the dead.

What comment can psychic science make upon such an episode? In the first place, I would judge that the miller was a powerful medium—that is, he exuded that rare atmosphere which enables a spirit to become visible as the meteorite becomes visible when it passes through the atmosphere of earth. It is, I repeat, a rare quality, and in this case seems to have been unknown to its possessor, though I should expect to find that the miller had many other psychic experiences which took a less public form. This is the reason why the appari- tion did not appear before the magistrate himself, but could only approach him by messenger. The spirit may have searched some time before she found her medium, just as Sergeant Davies was ten months before he found the Highlander who had those physical qualities which enabled him to communicate. Law and obedience to law run through the whole subject. It is also abundantly evident that the confiding woman who had been treated with such cold-blooded ingratitude and treachery carried over to the other world her natural feelings of indignation and her desire for justice. As a curious detail it is also evident that she recovered her conscious- ness instantly after death, and was enabled to observe the movements of her assassin. With what organs, one may ask? With what organs do we see clear details in a dream? There is something there besides our material eyes.

A most reasonable objection may be urged as to why many innocent people have suffered death and yet have experienced no super-normal help which might have saved them. Any criminologist could name off- hand a dozen cases where innocent men have gone to the scaffold. Why were they not saved? I have written in vain if I have not by now enabled the reader to answer the question himself. If the physical means are not there, then it is impossible. It may seem unjust, but not more so than the fact that a ship provided with wireless may save its passengers while another is heard of no more. The problem of unmerited suffering is part of that larger problem of the functions of pain and evil, which can only be explained on the supposition that spiritual chastening and elevation come in this fashion, and that this end is so important that the means are trivial in comparison. We must accept this provisional explanation, or we are faced with chaos.

Can these dim forces which we see looming above and around us be turned to the use of man? It would be a degradation to use them for purely material ends, and it would, in my opinion, bring some retribution with it; but, where the interests of Justice are concerned, I am convinced that they could indeed be used to good effect. Here is a case in point.

Two brothers, Eugene and Paul Dupont, lived some fifty years ago in the Rue St. Honoré of Paris. Eugene was a banker, Paul a man of letters. Eugene disappeared. Every conceivable effort was made to trace him, but the police finally gave it up as hopeless. Paul was persevering, however, in in company with a friend, Laporte, he visited Mme. Huerta, a well-known clairvoyante, and asked for her assistance.

We have no record as to how far articles of the missing man were given to the medium, as a bloodhound was started on a trail, but whether it was by psychometry or not, Mme. Huerta, in the mesmerized state, very quickly got in touch with the past of the two brothers, from the dinner where they had last met. She described Eugene, and followed his movements from the hour that he left the restaurant until he vanished into a house which was identified without difficulty by her audience, though she was unable to give the name of the street. She then described how inside the house Eugene Dupont had held a conference with two men whom she described, how he had signed some paper and had received a bundle of bank notes. She then saw him leave the house, she saw the two men follow him, she saw two other men join in their pursuit, and finally she saw the four assault the banker, murder him, and throw the body into the Seine.

Paul was convinced by the narrative, but his comrade, Laporte, regarded it as a fabrication. They had no sooner reached home, however, than they learned that the missing man had been picked out of the river and was exposed at the Morgue. The police, however, were inclined to take the view of suicide, as a good deal of money was in the pockets. Paul Dupont knew better, however. He hunted out the house, he discovered that the occupants did business with his brother's firm, he found that they held a receipt for two thousand pounds in exchange for notes paid to his brother on the night of the crime, and yet those notes were missing. A letter making an appointment was also discovered.

The two men, a father and son, named Dubuchet, were then arrested, and the missing links were at once discovered. The pocket-book which Eugene Dupont had in his possession on the night of the murder was found in Dubuchet's bureau. Other evidence was forthcoming, and finally the two villains were found guilty and were condemned to penal servitude for life. The medium was not summoned as a witness, on the ground that she was not conscious at the time of her vision, but her revelations undoubtedly brought about the discovery of the crime.

Now it is clear in this authentic case that the police would have saved themselves much trouble, and come to a swifter conclusion, had they themselves consulted Mme. Huerta in the first instance. And if it is obviously true in this case, why might it not be so in many other cases? It should be possible at every great police-centre to have the call upon the best clairvoyant or other medium that can be got, and to use them freely, for what they are worth. None are infallible. They have their off-days and their failures. No man should ever be convicted upon their evidence. But when it comes to suggesting clues and links, then it might be invaluable. In the case of Mr. Foxwell, the London stockbroker who fell into the Thames some years ago, it is well known that the mode of his death, and the place where his body would be found, were described by Von Bourg, the crystal-gazer, and that it was even as he had said. I venture to say that the mere knowledge that the police had an ally against whom every cunning precaution might prove unavailing would in itself be a strong deterrent to premeditated crime. This is so obvious, that if it had not been for vague scientific and religious prejudices, it would surely have been done long ago. Its adoption may be one of the first practical and material benefits given by psychic science to humanity.